SRA Reading Mastery

Signature Edition

Language Arts Workbook

Siegfried Engelmann
Jerry Silbert
Susan Hanner

McGraw Hill SRA

Columbus, OH

READING MASTERY® is a registered trademark of The McGraw-Hill Companies, Inc.

SRAonline.com

Send all inquiries to this address:
SRA/McGraw-Hill
4400 Easton Commons
Columbus, OH 43219

ISBN: 978-0-07-612609-5
MHID: 0-07-612609-9

11 12 13 14 15 HES 16 15 14 13

The McGraw·Hill Companies

A

1. The boy was from New York.	reports	does not report
2. A boy sat on the dock and fished.	reports	does not report
3. The boy wanted to be a boxer.	reports	does not report
4. The girl wore a red swimsuit.	reports	does not report
5. The girl sat in an inner tube.	reports	does not report
6. The girl liked to swim.	reports	does not report
7. The water was very warm.	reports	does not report
8. Several fish fell out of the bucket.	reports	does not report

B

1. jump _____   3. bark _____   5. pick _____

2. pull _____   4. push_____   6. burn _____

C

1. find	*found*	6. buy		11. dig	
2. give	*gave*	7. find		12. buy	
3. buy	*bought*	8. dig		13. has	
4. dig	*dug*	9. has		14. give	
5. has	*had*	10. give		15. find	

D

1. _____ ran into the room

2. _____ stood behind his desk

3. _____ made marks on a piece of paper

4. _____ watched the alligator from the front row

E Circle the part of each sentence that names.

An old cowboy went to town.

That cowboy rode his horse to town.

He went to town to buy food.

He rode his horse to the food store.

The cowboy went inside.

He bought the food that he needed.

F

	Part F
1.	Maria and her sister went to the store.
2.	My friend had a cold.
3.	The class went to the lunchroom.
4.	His bike had a flat tire.

A

1. Mrs. Lee talked to her sister.   reports   does not report

2. The baby sat on a rug.   reports   does not report

3. The baby had just learned how to walk.   reports   does not report

4. The cat reached toward the birdcage.   reports   does not report

5. The cat was seven years old.   reports   does not report

6. The dog liked to play with the baby.   reports   does not report

7. The baby held on to the dog's tail.   reports   does not report

8. Mrs. Lee was making a birthday cake.   reports   does not report

B Circle the part of each sentence that names.

A little gray cat looked for its owner. It looked and looked. The poor cat was hungry. The cat made a lot of noise. It went up one street and down another. The cat found its owner. That little cat felt very happy.

C Fill in each blank with *He, She* or *It.*

1. The car broke down.
2. The dream went on for an hour.
3. The young boy sat in a chair.
4. The monkey was laughing.
5. My older sister helped me.
6. The pen fell off the table.

1. _____ broke down.
2. _____ went on for an hour.
3. _____ sat in a chair.
4. _____ was laughing.
5. _____ helped me.
6. _____ fell off the table.

1.

The firefighter

- The firefighter is chopping a hole in the door.
- The firefighter was chopping a hole in the door.
- The firefighter chopped a hole in the door.

2.

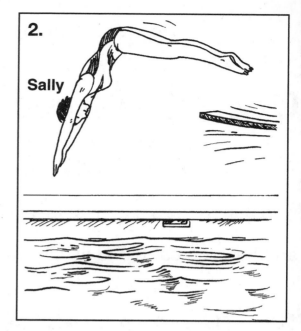

Sally

- Sally is diving into the pool.
- Sally dove into the pool.
- Sally was diving into the pool.

3.

Latrell

- Latrell ate a sandwich.
- Latrell was eating a sandwich.
- Latrell is eating a sandwich.

4.

The girl

- The girl was painting the wall.
- The girl is painting the wall.
- The girl painted the wall.

Lesson 2

E

1. The boy was eating lunch.

2. The girl is running home.

3. The boy was playing soccer.

4. He is drinking water.

5. She was driving a bus.

| drank | drove | ate | played | ran |

F

Part F

Pedro had a very smart dog. The dog could do many tricks. It could walk on its back legs. It could jump through a hoop. All of the children liked to play with the smart dog.

A Fill in each blank with *He, She* or *It.*

1. The shirt was covered with dirt.
2. The rubber ball fell off the table.
3. The man sat in a chair.
4. The book was very funny.
5. The young woman rode a bike.
6. The game ended at four o'clock.

1. _____ was covered with dirt.
2. _____ fell off the table.
3. _____ sat in a chair.
4. _____ was very funny.
5. _____ rode a bike.
6. _____ ended at four o'clock.

B Circle the part of each sentence that names.

An old red bike sat in the yard for years. That bike became rusty. It had spiderwebs on the wheels. A girl decided to fix up the bike. She painted the bike bright red. She put new tires on the bike. The bike looked great. The girl liked the bike.

C

A bull chased Pam through a field. Pam jumped over a fence. And then the bull jumped over the fence. And Pam kept on running. And the bull was right behind her. Pam ran over to a tree. And then she climbed up the tree as fast as she could. And the bull waited under the tree until the sun went down. And then Pam climbed down after the bull left. And she knew she shouldn't have taken a shortcut through that field.

D   Fix up each sentence so that it tells what the person or thing did.

1. He was taking a bath.

2. They were looking at the sky.

3. The dog was licking my face.

4. She is building a fire.

5. The teacher was sitting on a chair.

6. She is folding the paper.

built	folded	licked	looked	sat	took

 E

1. **Norma**

2. **Yancy**

- Norma was sawing a board.
- Norma is sawing a board.
- Norma sawed a board.

- Yancy was trying to ride a horse.
- Yancy tried to ride a horse.
- Yancy is trying to ride a horse.

F Write sentences that report on the main thing each person did.

1. James

2. A girl

3. Robert

| board | teeth | brushed | kicked | erased | football |

G

	Part G
	Jason had a bad day. He
	missed breakfast because he
	woke up late. He had to walk to
	school in the rain.
	1 ☐ 2 ☐ 3 ☐

Check 1: Does each sentence begin with a capital and end with a period?

Check 2: Did you spell all the words correctly?

Check 3: Did you indent the first line and start all the other lines at the margin?

A   Circle the part of each sentence that names.

A hungry little cat walked into a restaurant. It wanted something to eat.
A nice woman owned the restaurant. She gave the cat a bowl of milk.
The little animal drank every drop of milk. The woman liked the cat. She made
a little bed for it. The cat had a new home.

B

Tom threw a snowball at his friend. And it hit his friend's leg. And then his
friend chased him. And they both ran as fast as they could. His friend caught
Tom in the middle of the park. And then Tom told his friend that he was sorry
for hitting him in the leg with the snowball. The boys shook hands. And they
were still friends.

Lesson 4

C Fill in the blank next to each sentence with *He, She, It* or *They.*

1. The man and the woman ate lunch.

2. Latrell and Kedrick walked on the sand.

3. The truck had a flat tire.

4. The apples cost 84 cents.

5. The women wore red shirts.

6. The old book was worth a lot of money.

7. Alberto and his dog went jogging.

8. The old man wore a long blue coat.

1. _____ ate lunch.

2. _____ walked on the sand.

3. _____ had a flat tire.

4. _____ cost 84 cents.

5. _____ wore red shirts.

6. _____ was worth a lot of money.

7. _____ went jogging.

8. _____ wore a long blue coat.

D   Fix up each sentence so that it tells what the persons did.

1. She is riding a horse.

2. The girls were talking loudly.

3. The men are painting the room.

4. He was holding the baby.

5. She is standing on a chair.

6. They were washing the windows.

| held | painted | rode | stood | talked | washed |

E   Fix up the passage so that all the sentences tell what the person did.

Marcus woke up late. He was running down the stairs. He grabbed his school book. He is jumping onto his bike. He rode the bike as fast as he could. He was parking the bike. He ran into the classroom. He was sitting in his chair.

Lesson 5

 A Put in the capitals and periods. Circle the part of each sentence that names.

A young boy threw a ball the ball went over his friend's head it rolled into the street a big truck ran over the ball the truck driver gave the boys a new ball they thanked the truck driver

 B

1. The workers fixed the house and two carpenters nailed boards over the broken windows and a plumber repaired the broken sink.

2. The girls rode their bikes to school and their friends took the bus to school and everyone got to school on time.

3. The telephone rang six times and nobody heard it and everybody was outside in the yard.

C Fix up each sentence so that it tells what the persons did.

1. They were wearing helmets.

2. She was throwing the ball.

3. They were cleaning the room.

4. The boys were sitting on the floor.

5. He was wearing a new shirt.

6. The clown was rubbing his nose.

| sat | threw | rubbed | wore | cleaned |

14   *Lesson 5*

D   Fix up the passage so that all the sentences tell what the person did, not what the person was doing.

Jerry heard a noise. He was seeing a little kitten on the sidewalk. He

picked up the kitten. He was taking it home with him. He was giving it some

water. He made a little bed for it. He loved his new pet.

E   Fill in the blank next to each sentence with *He, She, It* or *They.*

1. A cat and a dog made a mess.

2. The girls went to school.

3. My mother was very pretty.

4. Rodney and his brother were not home.

5. Four ducks swam on the lake.

6. The tables were old.

7. My brother came home late.

8. That car was bright red.

1. _____ made a mess.

2. _____ went to school.

3. _____ was very pretty.

4. _____ were not home.

5. _____ swam on the lake.

6. _____ were old.

7. _____ came home late.

8. _____ was bright red.

DID	A bluebird sat on a tree branch. A striped cat was running up the trunk of the tree to get the bird. The cat ran
CP	toward the bird The bird flew away.
M	The branch broke. The cat held out its paws

Check 1: Does each sentence tell the main thing? (M)

Check 2: Does each sentence begin with a capital and end with a period? (CP)

Check 3: Does each sentence tell what somebody or something did? (DID)

A Put in the capitals and periods.

	a boy took his mom to the movies he had
	a good time the movie was very funny
	his mom bought a big box of popcorn they
	rode home on their bikes

B Fix up the passage so that no sentence begins with *and* or *and then.*

Richard had a good day. Richard's teacher gave Richard his report card just before the school day ended. And Richard jumped with joy when he saw the good marks on his report card. And then he ran home to show his mother the report card. And then he gave her the report card. And then his mother read the report card for several minutes. And she was so happy that she made Richard and the rest of the children a big pizza for dinner.

C   Fix up the run-on sentences.

1. The boy ran down the street and he held his books in his arms.

2. The girl ran into the room and she looked all over for her books and she didn't know where they could be.

3. The airplane flew above the clouds and it was about 60 miles from the airport and the pilot looked at the charts.

4. The boy walked slowly to the store and he stopped three times to talk to his friends and the store was closed when the boy got there.

5. Rosa wrote a funny story about alligators and she read it to the class and the children liked her story very much.

6. The dog did a trick and it walked in circles on its back legs and the boy gave the dog a snack for doing such a good trick.

D   Fix up each sentence so that it tells what the person or thing did.

1. The boy was chasing a dog.

2. The girl was washing the car.

3. He was writing a letter.

4. She was eating apples.

5. The airplane was taking off.

| took | chased | wrote | ate | washed |

E   Circle the subject. Underline the part that tells more.

1. Three older boys went to the store.

2. A horse and a dog went to a stream.

3. A man sat on a log.

4. They sat on a bench.

5. My friend and his mother were hungry.

6. My hands and my face got dirty.

Lesson 7

A   Put in the capitals and periods.

	a girl threw a ball to her brother she
	threw the ball too hard it rolled into the
	street the boy started to run into the
	street a truck moved toward the boy a
	woman saw the truck she grabbed the boy
	the truck ran over the ball the woman told
	the boy to be more careful

B   Fill in the blanks with **He, She** or **It.**

1. Robert spent all morning cleaning his room. _____ put his dirty clothes into the laundry basket. _____ washed the floor and the windows.

2. My sister went to the park. _____ played basketball with her friends for two hours. _____ scored 20 points.

3. The boat went around the small lake. _____ had three sails. _____ moved very quickly across the water.

1. Alberto ate lunch in the kitchen and he ate two cheese sandwiches covered with mustard and he got mustard all over his face and shirt.

2. The girl looked out the window at the snow and she did not like cold weather and she wished that she lived in a warmer place.

3. The dog ran down the street and it barked at a truck and the truck driver waved at the dog.

4. My friend did not feel well and she had a fever and her mother kept her home from school.

5. The dish fell off the table and it broke into many pieces and the boy swept up the pieces.

6. Rodney listened to the voice on the telephone and he didn't know who was speaking and the voice sounded strange.

D Fix up each sentence so that it tells what the person did.

1. The men were telling jokes.

2. She was picking up the pencils.

3. They were washing the car.

4. He was sitting on a log.

5. She was painting the wall.

painted	told	sat	washed	picked

Lesson 7

 Circle the subject of each sentence. Underline the part that tells more.

1. A jet airplane made a lot of noise.
2. A man and his dog went walking.
3. He ate lunch in the office.
4. My brother and his friend played in the park.
5. A little cat drank milk.

F

CP	*A cowboy fell off a bull. a bull charged*
DID	*at the cowboy. A clown was putting a*
M	*barrel in front of the bull. ^ The clown*
	helped the cowboy walk away from the bull.

Check 1: Does each sentence tell the main thing? (M)
Check 2: Does each sentence begin with a capital and end with a period? (CP)
Check 3: Does each sentence tell what somebody or something did? (DID)

A   Fix up the run-on sentences in this passage.

A girl got a big dog for her birthday and the dog was so big that it could not fit through the doors of the girl's house. It had to live outside in a house with big doors. The dog followed the girl to the school bus stop one morning and the girl didn't see the dog behind her and the dog tried to sneak onto the bus. The door of the bus was too small. The dog got stuck and all the children had to push together to get the dog off the bus.

B   Fix up the passage so that each sentence begins with a capital and ends with a period.

	a man took a big egg out of a nest. The
	man brought the egg to his house he
	thought that the egg might be worth a lot
	of money. The doorbell rang the man walked
	to the door. He opened the door a big bird
	flew into the room. It picked up the egg
	the man fainted. The big bird flew away with
	the egg

Lesson 8

C Edit the passage for these checks:

Check 1: Do any sentences begin with *and* or *and then?*

Check 2: Do all the words that are part of a person's name begin with a capital?

tonya jackson was playing baseball. And her team was losing two to one. tonya was at bat. The pitcher threw the ball to tonya. tonya swung. She missed the ball. And tonya was mad. The pitcher threw the ball toward Tonya again. And then Tonya swung. She hit the ball. And it went far over everybody's head. Tonya ran around the bases. Her team won the game. And then all the girls clapped for tonya.

D Cross out some of the names and write *He, She* or *It.*

Ⓐ Mario found many things when he went walking. Ⓑ Mario once found a striped cat. Ⓒ That cat was very thin. Ⓓ That cat was sitting on the sidewalk. Ⓔ Mario took the cat home with him. Ⓕ Mario tried to hide the cat from his mother. Ⓖ His mother heard the cat. Ⓗ His mother liked the cat and told Mario that he could keep it.

E   Circle the subject of each sentence. Underline the predicate.

1. Five cats were on the roof.

2. They read two funny books.

3. A red bird landed on a roof.

4. A dog and a cat played in their yard.

5. It stopped.

A Fix up the run-on sentences in this passage.

Tom made some chocolate cookies and he put them in a shoe box and he put the shoe box in a corner of the kitchen. He went outside to play. Susan started cleaning the kitchen and she did not know what was in the shoe box and she threw the shoe box away. Tom got hungry. He went into the kitchen. He looked for the shoe box. It was gone. He asked Susan if she had seen the shoe box and she told him she had thrown it away. Tom told Susan what was in the shoe box. Susan helped Tom make another batch of cookies.

B Cross out some of the names and write *He, She* or *It.*

(A) Trina loved to look for things on the sidewalk. (B) Trina found three bugs, two rocks and a baseball yesterday. (C) Her father did not like some of the things she found. (D) Her father did not like the bugs that Trina brought home. (E) Trina's brother liked one of the things Trina found. (F) Trina's brother liked the baseball.

C Fix up the passage so that each sentence begins with a capital and ends with a period.

	a man saw a butterfly it had purple and white spots. The man wanted to catch the butterfly he got a net. He started to chase the butterfly it flew over a pond. The man fell into the pond the pretty butterfly flew away

D If the words are somebody's name, begin the words with capital letters.

lamar jenkins	mrs. williams	the doctor	his brother
tyrell washington	jerry martinez	this boy	mr. garcia
	the girl	the nurse	mrs. cash

E Fix up the passage so that all the sentences tell what a person did, not what a person was doing.

Shameka bought a little tree. She was digging a hole in her yard. She put the tree into the hole. She was filling the hole with dirt. She was watering the tree. She built a little fence around the tree.

F   Circle the subject of each sentence. Underline the predicate.

1. Sara and Harry painted the kitchen blue.
2. Sara had a paintbrush.
3. Harry used a roller.
4. They stopped to eat lunch.
5. She laughed.
6. The windows were blue.

G

DID	Jill threw a ball to Robert. Robert jump up to catch the ball. The ball went over
CP	Robert's head it rolled down the hill toward a skunk. Rover chased the ball.
M	^ Robert and Jill held their noses.

Check 1: Does each sentence tell the main thing? (M)
Check 2: Does each sentence begin with a capital and end with a period? (CP)
Check 3: Does each sentence tell what somebody or something did? (DID)

A Fix up the run-on sentences.

1. Mr. Clark went for a ride in the country and then his car ran out of gas and then he had to walk three miles to a gas station.

2. Kathy liked to read books and her favorite book was about horses and her brother gave her that book.

3. Pam's mother asked Pam to mow the lawn and then Pam started to cut the grass and it was too wet.

B Cross out some of the names, and write *he, she* or *it.*

James had a birthday yesterday. James was 11 years old. His mother brought a big birthday cake to school. His mother gave a piece of cake to each person in James' class. The cake tasted great. The cake had chocolate icing.

Test Score [ ]

A Put in the capitals and periods.

My older sister took her dog to the park her dog chased a skunk the skunk got mad it made a terrible stink my sister had to wash her dog for hours to get rid of the smell

B Fix up the sentences so they tell what people did.

1. He was giving me a pen.

2. He was buying a shirt.

3. They were picking flowers.

4. He is filling the glass.

5. My friend is having a party.

6. A boy is spelling words.

gave	bought

C   Fill in the blanks with **He, She, It** or **They.**

1. Two girls ate lunch.

2. A cow and a horse slept in the barn.

3. His sister went home.

4. The blue pen fell off the desk.

5. James is sick today.

6. My friends went to a party.

1. _____ ate lunch.

2. _____ slept in the barn.

3. _____ went home.

4. _____ fell off the desk.

5. _____ is sick today.

6. _____ went to a party.

D   Circle the subject of each sentence. Underline the predicate.

1. A young man walked home.

2. It made a big noise.

3. My little sister is sick.

4. Her brother and sister went to school.

5. That pencil belongs to her.

    Lesson 10—Test 1   **31**

A   Fill in the blanks with the correct words.

Three women worked on a house.

_____ wore work clothes.

_____ cut a board. _____

used a saw. _____ carried three

pieces of wood. _____ carried the

boards on her shoulder. _____

hammered nails into the wood.

B   Fix up the run-on sentences.

1. Miss Wilson saw a used bike at a store and the bike was red and blue
   and then Miss Wilson bought it for her sister. (3)

2. Richard and his sister went to a movie and it was very funny and Richard
   and his sister ate popcorn and then their mother picked them up after the
   movie. (4)

3. Tina built a doghouse for her dog and then she looked in the doghouse
   and four cats were in the doghouse with her dog. (3)

Circle the subject of each sentence. Underline the predicate.
Then make a **V** above the verb.

1. Six bottles were on the table.

2. An old lion chased the rabbit.

3. Jane and Sue sat under a tree.

4. His brother had a candy bar.

D

A woman lived near our school Her name was mrs. jones she was an

airplane pilot. She told us many stories about flying planes

☐ **Check 1.** Does each sentence begin with a capital and end with a
period?
☐ **Check 2.** Does each part of a person's name begin with a capital letter?

A

1. A black pencil fell off the table.

2. My sister was sick.

3. A dog and a cat played in the park.

4. They smiled.

5. Mary sang softly.

6. An old horse drank from a bucket.

B Fix up the run-on sentences in this paragraph.

Don found a lost dog and the dog had a collar around its neck. The collar had a phone number on it and then Don called the phone number and the dog's owner answered the telephone. The owner was happy that Don found the dog. He went to Don's house and then Don gave the dog to the owner.

C For each verb that tells what somebody does, write the verb that tells what somebody did.

1. begins _____

2. brings _____

3. flies _____

4. swims _____

5. takes _____

6. comes _____

D Fill in the blanks with the correct words.

_____ sat in the

wheelchair. _____ wore pajamas.

The _____ had big wheels and

little wheels. _____ had a seat,

a back and two handles. _____

held a purse. _____ wore a skirt

and a sweater. _____ was behind

the wheelchair. _____ pushed the wheelchair.

Ruth Ben Dora wheelchair

E

	A little bird fell out of its nest.
DID	James pick up the little bird. His
M	sister climbed up the tree. ^
CP	she put the bird back in its nest.

Check 1: Does each sentence tell the main thing? (M)
Check 2: Does each sentence begin with a capital and end with a period? (CP)
Check 3: Does each sentence tell what somebody or something did? (DID)

A

1. She jumped into the pool.

2. A young woman read a book about dinosaurs.

3. My mother had a new car.

4. They laughed.

5. My brother and my sister ate cookies and ice cream.

B

Linda went on an airplane and she had never been on an airplane before. She sat in a seat next to the window and the plane took off. She fell asleep for an hour and she woke up and the plane landed. Her grandmother was waiting for her.

C Fill in the blanks with the correct words.

_____ and _____ worked

in the garden. _____ wore work

clothes. _____ dug a hole.

_____ pushed the shovel down with

her foot. _____ sawed a branch.

_____ held the branch with one

hand.

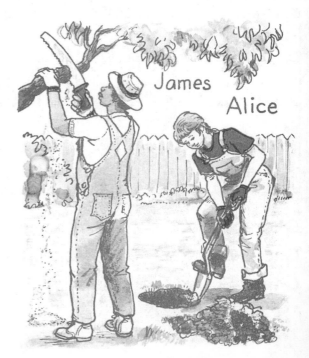

James

Alice

A   Fix up the run-on sentences in the paragraph.

     Jessica and Mark bought a pumpkin for Halloween and the pumpkin was so big that they could not carry it home. They started to roll it home. They pushed the pumpkin up a steep hill and then Mark slipped. The pumpkin rolled down the hill. It smashed into a tree and Jessica and Mark had lots of pumpkin pie the next day.

B

1. walked   2. smiled   3. picked   4. cried

   was walking

C   Write the missing word in each item.

1. the hat that belongs to the boy   the ___*boy's*___ hat

2. the bone that belongs to the dog   the _____ bone

3. the car that belongs to her father   her _____ car

4. the arm that belongs to the girl   the _____ arm

5. the book that belongs to my friend   my _____ book

6. the toy that belongs to the cat   the _____ toy

D

| corner | licking | floor | boy's hand | sitting |

Circle the name of each thing that is different in picture 1 and picture 2.

the glass   bowl of fruit   boy   pajamas

cat   milk in the glass   wall

A Fix up the run-on sentences in the paragraph.

     Ronald put his finger in a bottle and his finger got stuck in the bottle and then he asked his sister to help him. His sister got some butter and then she rubbed the butter around the top of the bottle. She pulled on the bottle and then his finger came out.

B Circle the subject. Underline the predicate. Make a **V** above every verb.

1. The boy walked to the store.

   The boy was walking to the store.

2. Two girls ate candy.

   Two girls were eating candy.

3. A fish swam in the bathtub.

   A fish was swimming in the bathtub.

C Write the missing word in each item.

1. the dress that belongs to the girl   the __*girl's*__ dress

2. the tent that belongs to her friend   her _____ tent

3. the toy that belongs to my cat   my _____ toy

4. the watch that belongs to that boy   that _____ watch

5. the hammer that belongs to his mother   his _____ hammer

6. the leg that belongs to my father   my_____ leg

1. Steve bent down and picked up a pencil.

2. Three girls watched a movie and ate popcorn.

3. He brushed his teeth and washed his face.

| lying | sitting | horse | ground | running away |

1.

2.

Circle the name of each thing that is different in picture 1 and picture 2.

the horse   boy   boy's hat   cowboy

the cowboy's hat   mountain

B   Circle the subject. Underline the predicate. Make a **V** above every verb.

1. The young woman walked to the school.

    The young woman was walking to the school.

2. The children smiled at the clown.

    The children were smiling at the clown.

3. Mark and Jenny raked the leaves.

    Mark and Jenny were raking the leaves.

4. They swam in the lake.

    They were swimming in the lake.

C   Fix up the run-on sentences.

1. The boy went to the store and bought groceries.

2. The boy went to the store and then his sister bought groceries.

3. My brother mowed the lawn and swept the sidewalk.

4. My brother mowed the lawn and then he swept the sidewalk later.

5. The workers started early and their boss went home late.

6. The workers started early and went home late.

7. She ran up the stairs and went inside the house.

8. She ran up the stairs and she went inside.

1. The shirt belonged to **that boy.** The shirt was red.

   _____ was red.

2. The tail belonged to **a lion.** The tail was long.

   _____ was long.

3. The desk belonged to **my teacher.** The desk was old.

   _____ was old.

4. The hand belonged to **his mother.** The hand was sore.

   _____ was sore.

5. The car belonged to **my sister.** The car was dented.

   _____ was dented.

E

CP	*A truck went over a rock*
	A barrel fell out of the truck. The
DID	*barrel roll down a hill. It crashed*
WH	*into a tree. ^ The boy caught the*
RO	*apple and he gave it to a teacher.*

Check 1: Did you give a clear picture of what happened? (WH)

Check 2: Did you fix up any run-on sentences? (RO)

Check 3: Does each sentence begin with a capital and end with a period? (CP)

Check 4: Does each sentence tell what somebody or something did? (DID)

Lesson 16   **43**

Lesson 17

A   Fix up the run-on sentences.

1. Melissa fed her dog and she went inside to change her shoes.

2. Ann loved horses and her big brother wanted a horse for his birthday.

3. The children went to the farm and played with the animals.

4. My brother swept the floor and washed the dishes.

5. A man and a woman watched TV and he had a sore arm.

6. Ron went to the park and fed the birds.

B   Rewrite each item with an apostrophe **s.**

1. The pencil belonged to **a girl.** The pencil was yellow.

   _____ was yellow.

2. The nest belonged to **that bird.** The nest had eggs in it.

   _____ had eggs in it.

3. The glasses belonged to **my friend.** The glasses were broken.

   _____ were broken.

4. The bottle belonged to **her baby.** The bottle had milk in it.

   _____ had milk in it.

C Write sentences that tell what must have happened in the middle
picture. Tell about **the candle, the newspapers** and **the woman.**

| bucket | fell | burn |

Lesson 18

A   Fix up the run-on sentences in this paragraph.

Tom stopped in front of the pet shop and looked in the window. He saw a puppy inside and the pet store was open and Tom didn't have any money to buy the puppy. He wanted the puppy and he went home to talk to his parents. They told him he could have the puppy. Tom did jobs and then he earned the money he needed to buy the puppy

B   Rewrite each item with an apostrophe **s.**

1. The car belonged to **Tom.** The car was new.

_____ was new.

2. The wheel belonged to **his bike.** The wheel was bent.

_____ was bent.

3. The motor belonged to **that truck.** The motor made a lot of noise.

_____ made a lot of noise.

4. The finger belonged to **Sally.** The finger was swollen.

_____ was swollen.

5. The mouth belonged to **the dog.** The mouth was sore.

_____ was sore.

46   *Lesson 18*

C Write sentences that tell what must have happened in the middle picture. Tell about **the horse, Bill** and **Lisa.**

| corral | grabbed | fence | rail |

D

RO	*A gorilla escaped from its cage and the*
	zookeeper made a trail of bananas that led
DID	*back to the cage. The gorilla follow the*
	zookeeper. It picked up the bananas and
WH	*started to eat them. ^ The zookeeper*
	closed the gate behind the gorilla.

Check 1: Did you give a clear picture of what happened? (WH)

Check 2: Did you fix up any run-on sentences? (RO)

Check 3: Does each sentence begin with a capital and end with a period? (CP)

Check 4: Does each sentence tell what somebody or something did? (DID)

Lesson 18 **47**

A Write sentences that tell what must have happened in the middle picture. Tell about **the baker, the flyswatter, the pie** and **the fly.**

| pie | flyswatter | swung | flew away | splattered |

A

RO	Alex threw a frisbee to his dog and the
	frisbee went over the dog's head. A bear cub
WH	grabbed the frisbee. The mother bear
DID	heard the barking and walk into the
	field. Alex picked up his dog and ran to
CP	a big tree

Check 1: Did you give a clear picture of what happened? (WH)

Check 2: Did you fix up any run-on sentences? (RO)

Check 3: Does each sentence begin with a capital and end with a period? (CP)

Check 4: Does each sentence tell what somebody or something did? (DID)

TEST 2

Test Score [ ]

A   Read the paragraph. Fix up any run-ons.

     A turtle and a rabbit had a race and the rabbit ran very fast. The turtle could not run fast. The rabbit saw a garden full of carrots and then the rabbit stopped and ate lots of carrots. The turtle kept on running and the turtle won the race and then the rabbit got mad because he lost the race.

B   Write the verb for each sentence.

1. The red pencil fell on the floor. _____

2. My little brother was sleeping under the bed. _____

3. The bus had eight wheels. _____

4. My brother and my sister were running up the stairs. _____

5. They stopped. _____

6. We found a little dog. _____

C   Rewrite each item with an apostrophe **s.**

1. The shirt belonged to **Tom.** The shirt was dirty.

_____ was dirty.

2. The dog belonged to **his sister.** The dog was barking.

_____ was barking.

3. The toy belonged to **the baby.** The toy was on the bed.

_____ was on the bed.

4. The motor belonged to **that car.** The motor made a loud noise.

_____ made a loud noise.

D   Fill in the blanks with the correct words.

The men went fishing. _____

were in a boat in the middle of the lake.

_____ sat in the middle of the

boat. _____ held a fishing pole

in one hand and a net in the other hand.

_____ sat in the back of the boat.

_____ stood in the front of the boat.

_____ smiled as his fishing pole bent.

1. Milly played baseball with Linda. Milly / She threw the ball.

2. Milly played baseball with Jeff. Milly / She threw the ball.

3. Gary and John went to the store. John / He had been working all day.

4. Jessica talked to Liz. Jessica / She was walking home.

5. Kathy handed a glass to Bill. Kathy / She told him where to put it.

B Circle all the words in column 4 that are verbs.

1	2	3	4
ran	girls	cried	went
talked	stove	bought	bird
turned	brother	house	walked
yelled	pretty	whispered	flew
sat	quietly	teacher	pretty
smiled	man	yellow	slept
fell	lazy	swam	sold

A

1. Tom waved to Martha. $\overset{\text{Martha}}{\text{She}}$ was riding a horse.

2. Larry wanted to meet James. $\overset{\text{Larry}}{\text{He}}$ had a new bike.

3. Barbara gave her sister a rabbit. $\overset{\text{Her sister}}{\text{She}}$ loved rabbits.

4. Mr. Ross and Mr. Long were teachers. $\overset{\text{Mr. Ross}}{\text{He}}$ taught math.

5. Bill went fishing with Linda. $\overset{\text{Linda}}{\text{She}}$ caught four fish.

6. Ann and her mother went to a party. $\overset{\text{Ann}}{\text{She}}$ carried a cake.

B

1. six <u>chairs</u>

2. my fathers <u>chairs</u>

3. my fathers <u>chair</u>

4. some <u>apples</u>

5. that trees <u>leaves</u>

6. a cars <u>headlights</u>

7. a boys <u>kites</u>

8. two big <u>oranges</u>

9. those red <u>cars</u>

10. that boys <u>books</u>

11. the teachers <u>pencil</u>

12. the tallest <u>girls</u>

C   Circle each word that is a verb.

bought   smiled   green   tall   kicked   went   boy

Lesson 23

A

1. Wendy and Debbie went to the beach. $\begin{array}{c}\text{Wendy}\\\text{She}\end{array}$ flew her kite.

2. Robert and Dave walked home. $\begin{array}{c}\text{Dave}\\\text{He}\end{array}$ carried a radio.

3. Tom and Pam walked to school. $\begin{array}{c}\text{Pam}\\\text{She}\end{array}$ liked to walk fast.

4. Ed and Sam talked in the hall. $\begin{array}{c}\text{Ed}\\\text{He}\end{array}$ stood near the door.

5. Linda helped Alice build a table. $\begin{array}{c}\text{Linda}\\\text{She}\end{array}$ wanted to paint it red.

6. Ed asked Bob about school. $\begin{array}{c}\text{Ed}\\\text{He}\end{array}$ had been absent for a week.

B

1. a girls <u>hairbrush</u>

2. that cats <u>tail</u>

3. the birds in the <u>tree</u>

4. the bugs on the <u>table</u>

5. those cats near <u>John</u>

6. an old mans <u>face</u>

7. the womans <u>umbrella</u>

8. many <u>cups</u>

9. a girls <u>suitcase</u>

1. Bill and Frank ate lunch. ~~Bill~~ He had a peanut butter sandwich.

2. Miss Winston and Miss Kelly were teachers. ~~Miss Kelly~~ She taught reading.

3. Kevin told Ann about a movie. ~~Kevin~~ He thought it was very funny.

4. My father gave Betty a book. ~~Betty~~ She liked to read books about space.

5. Tina sat next to Jane. ~~Tina~~ She was the smartest girl in class.

6. Wendy worked with Bill. ~~Wendy~~ She fixed a flat tire.

B Change each sentence so the subject is a pronoun. Cross out the subject. Write the pronoun above it.

1. The old man could not start the car.

2. A storm lasted all night.

3. A dog and a cow were eating.

4. The young woman cleaned a table.

5. The trucks went up the hill.

6. A mother held a baby.

A Circle the subject in each sentence. Write **P** in front of every sentence that has a pronoun for a subject.

_____ 1. Donald planted corn.

_____ 2. It had a broken handle.

_____ 3. He kicked a football.

_____ 4. Betty baked three pies.

_____ 5. The truck had 16 wheels.

_____ 6. They woke up late.

_____ 7. She planted corn.

_____ 8. Bugs ran all over the table.

B

_____ and _____ were swimming. _____ wore a bathing cap. _____ also wore a watch. _____ sat near the water. _____ wore sunglasses.

_____ stood next to the blanket.

_____ wore shorts. _____ read a book.

C

1. the boys goed to Bills house. (3)

2. Alice fell asleep she was very tired. (2)

3. that boys shirt has six red buttons and four yellow buttons (3)

4. My best friends are jerry gomez and alex jordan. (4)

5. Melissa and richard put their dog on richards bed. (3)

6. We looked outside and The rain had just stopped. (2)

A Circle the subject in each sentence. Write **P** in front of every sentence that has a pronoun for a subject.

_____ 1. The tree was beautiful.   _____ 5. It fell off the table.

_____ 2. He ate pizza for dinner.   _____ 6. They bought new shirts.

_____ 3. Those dogs chased our cat.   _____ 7. My sister painted the room.

_____ 4. Tina read a book.   _____ 8. Robert finished his homework.

B

_____ and _____ picked apples from a tree.

_____ wore a hat. _____ had a beard. _____ stood on

a box. _____ held a bucket. _____ and _____ sat on a

blanket. _____ read a book. _____ wore a shirt with the

number 9 on the back. _____ drew a picture.

C

1. My dads cat had four kittens (2)

2. She teached robert and jerry how to ride a bike. (3)

3. she washed the windows of her dads car (3)

4. We seen mrs. jordan in the store she waved to us. (5)

Ⓐ Circle the subject in each sentence. Write **P** in front of each sentence that has a pronoun for a subject.

_____ 1. Linda's shirt was dirty.

_____ 2. They painted the door.

_____ 3. He is ten years old.

_____ 4. A new girl walked into our class.

_____ 5. It had big tires.

_____ 6. A boy and his friend went to the store.

_____ 7. My little brother is seven years old.

_____ 8. She walked to school.

Ⓑ

_____ and _____ were playing basketball.

_____ bounced a ball. _____ wore shorts and long socks.

_____ wore a headband to keep her hair from getting in her eyes.

_____ jumped into the air as she shot the ball toward the basket.

_____ leaned against a pole as she watched the girls play basketball.

_____ read a newspaper. _____ sat on a bench.

1. Ann walked to school with Jenny. A car splashed water on Ann. her.

2. Randy and Steve ran down the street. A black cat ran in front of Steve. him.

3. Tom saw Nancy at the store. The clerk was giving Nancy her change.

4. Frank talked to Peter. Everybody liked Peter. him.

5. Beth went swimming with Mike. She splashed water at Mike. him.

1. He went to the store after dinner.

2. She fell asleep before the movie ended.

3. A bird started to sing early in the morning.

4. The boy cleaned the garage after breakfast.

5. Ann fixed her car yesterday.

6. All the people clapped when the movie ended.

Lesson 29

A

1. Don and Mark raked leaves. Carol gave ~~Don~~ him a bag for the leaves.

2. Mr. Swift fixed lunch for Miss Adams. He gave ~~Miss Adams~~ her a large bowl of soup.

3. Linda wanted to be a clown for Halloween. Steve found a funny outfit for ~~Linda~~ her to wear.

4. Tina and Alice waited in the doctor's office. The nurse told ~~Alice~~ her to go into the room.

5. Jeff and Kurt left school. Mr. Dukes gave ~~Kurt~~ him a ride home.

B

1. Two trees fell down during the storm.

2. The baby started to cry when his mother left the room.

3. Tom finished his homework at eleven o'clock in the morning.

4. The boy cleaned his room while his mother went shopping.

5. They shook hands after the game.

6. We went to the movies last night.

TEST 3

Test Score [ ]

A The number after each item tells how many mistakes in the item. Fix up the mistakes.

1. the boys goed to Bills house. (3)

2. Alice fell asleep she was very tired. (2)

3. that boys shirt has six red buttons and four yellow buttons (3)

4. My best friends are jerry gomez and alex jordan. (4)

5. Melissa and richard put their dog on richards bed. (3)

6. We looked outside and The rain had just stopped. (2)

B Fill in the blanks.

_____ and _____

were swimming. _____ wore a

bathing cap. _____ also wore a

watch. _____ sat near the

water. _____ wore sunglasses.

_____ stood next to the blanket.

_____ wore shorts. _____

read a book.

TEST 3

C Circle the subject in each sentence.
Write **P** in front of every sentence that has a pronoun for a subject.

_____ 1. Donald planted corn.

_____ 2. It had a broken handle.

_____ 3. He kicked a football.

_____ 4. Betty baked three pies.

_____ 5. The truck had 16 wheels.

_____ 6. They woke up late.

_____ 7. She planted corn.

_____ 8. Bugs ran all over the table.

D Put in an apostrophe if the words tell that the underlined object belongs to someone.

1. a girls <u>hairbrush</u>

2. that cats <u>tail</u>

3. the birds in the <u>tree</u>

4. the bugs on the <u>table</u>

5. an old mans <u>face</u>

6. the womans <u>umbrella</u>

7. many <u>cups</u>

8. a girls <u>suitcase</u>

A

1. He brushed his teeth after he washed his face.

2. James and Tom did their math in the morning.

3. The engine made a funny noise before the car stopped.

4. Tom read a book while he waited for his brother.

5. Alice and her mother went shopping yesterday afternoon.

6. Our teacher read a story during the lunch hour.

7. The clown climbed the rope when a bell rang.

8. Smoke came from the house after lightning hit it.

B
Write each sentence with the correct punctuation.
Make sure you follow these punctuation rules:
    a. Put a comma after the word **said.**
    b. Capitalize the first word the person said.
    c. Put a period or a question mark after the last word the person
       said.
    d. Put quote marks around the exact words the person said.

1. She said why are you so happy

2. He said the sun is shining

3. Tim said do you have a pencil

4. Alice said my pencil is broken

Lesson 31

A

1. Our dog barked when the door opened.

2. We went shopping last night.

3. The girls painted the room while the boys washed the car.

4. Everybody fell asleep after lunch.

5. He held his nose as he jumped into the water.

6. Nobody talked during the movie.

B Write **V** above each **verb.** Write **P** above each **pronoun.**

1. <u>It</u> <u>was landing</u> on the runway.
     1   2

2. <u>They</u> wheeled <u>it</u> into the store.
     3   4

3. The dog <u>barked</u> loudly at <u>him</u>.
            5   6

4. <u>He</u> <u>forgot</u> his homework.
     7   8

A

1. John went home after the party.
2. After the party, John went home.

3. The girls were tired by the time the sun went down.
4. By the time the sun went down, the girls were tired.

5. The engine made a funny noise before the car stopped.
6. Before the car stopped, the engine made a funny noise.

7. Tammy listened to the radio while Bill did his homework.
8. While Bill did his homework, Tammy listened to the radio.

B

1. Tom said, "why did you do that? (2)

2. They seen fred and jerry at the store. (3)

3. Maria said "i love math." (2)

4. Lisa teached Marys brother to swim. (2)

5. My sister went to the doctor and she had a cold. (3)

A Circle the subject.
Underline the whole predicate.
Make a line over the part that tells when.

1. Jane got a lot of work done while the baby slept.

   While the baby slept, Jane got a lot of work done.

2. The birds flew south in September.

   In September, the birds flew south.

3. She woke up before the alarm clock rang.

   Before the alarm clock rang, she woke up.

4. He worked on his boat every night.

   Every night, he worked on his boat.

B

1. The dogs chased the cats. I watched $\frac{\text{the cats}}{\text{them}}$ climb up a tree.

2. The boys and girls cleaned the house. $\frac{\text{The boys}}{\text{They}}$ washed the windows.

3. The rabbits ran under the fence. $\frac{\text{The rabbits}}{\text{They}}$ wanted the carrots.

2. Linda spoke to the boys. She told $\frac{\text{the boys}}{\text{them}}$ about the test.

5. He washed the forks and spoons. He put $\frac{\text{the forks}}{\text{them}}$ on the table.

A

1. Jane walked home after school.

   After school Jane walked home.

2. Tom read a book in the evening.

   In the evening, Tom read a book.

3. The girl rubbed her eyes when the lights came on.

   When the lights came on, the girl rubbed her eyes.

B

1. Sally had pencils and pens. She gave   the pens   to her friend.
           them

2. Tony found two kittens. He gave   the kittens   some milk.
           them

3. We saw bears and elephants.   The elephants   were eating peanuts.
           They

4. The boys and girls played baseball.   The girls   won the game.
           They

C

1. They said we are hungry. (4)

2. She teached jerry to cook. (2)

3. I said "are you tired? (3)

4. The bus went up the hill it made lots of noise. (2)

5. Jeff made dinner and he made a pie for dessert (4)

A Write **N** above the noun in each subject.

1. Dark clouds covered the sky.

2. An old dog slept on the floor.

3. The trucks got dirty.

4. Her little bike cost a lot of money.

5. My sister walked to school.

B

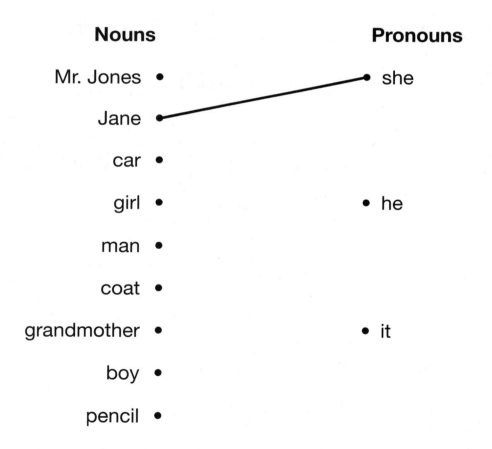

Nouns	Pronouns
Mr. Jones •	• she
Jane •	
car •	
girl •	• he
man •	
coat •	
grandmother •	• it
boy •	
pencil •	

A

girl •   • it

truck •

Tom •

apple •   • her

sister •

uncle •

Linda •   • him

light •

boy •

B

_____1. He fell asleep on the floor.

_____2. A big bird flew into the nest.

_____3. Alice came home early.

_____4. It made a big noise.

_____5. The young man started to speak.

_____6. Those girls are my sisters.

A

_____1. A broken bottle was on the floor.

_____2. It cost too much.

_____3. She is older than her sister.

_____4. That invention was very helpful.

_____5. Frogs make funny noises.

_____6. They are sleeping.

B

1. James said, Today is my birthday. We are having a party. (2)

2. Bill met Alice in the park. She said you look good. (4)

3. Anns dad is very tall he plays basketball. (3)

4. The doctor said you have a bad cold. Don't go outside. (4)

5. I seen ann and jane at Mr. jordans house. (5)

Write **N** above each noun.
Write **P** above each pronoun.
Write **V** above each verb.

1. Six <u>rabbits</u> <u>played</u> on <u>it</u>.

2. <u>Tom</u> <u>looked</u> at <u>them</u>.

3. <u>They</u> <u>talked</u> to <u>him</u> after lunch.

4. The <u>meeting</u> <u>made</u> <u>her</u> mad.

5. <u>She</u> <u>saw</u> <u>it</u> when she came home.

6. A big <u>dog</u> <u>was</u> with <u>her</u>.

B   Put in the correct ending mark.

1. When did you go home

2. You can go to the movies

3. Did you find your hat

4. My brother is sick

5. That dog is mean

6. Can you come with us

7. Is your dog in the house

C

1. He said I can't find my dog. Have you seen him? (3)

2. She can drive a car and her brother taught her to drive. (3)

3. Linda adams and chris jordan were in my class (4)

4. James said, "where is Toms shirt? He wants it back. (3)

5. My brother was sick he had a bad cold. (2)

A

1. The boys went home after school.

2. During the rainstorm our dog hid under the bed.

3. After we fixed the car we made dinner.

4. In the morning Jane walked to school.

5. That girl was happy when she got her report card.

6. He fell asleep while he read a book.

7. After James sat down the music started.

B   Put in the correct ending mark.

1. Where is Tom

2. Tom and Sally went home

3. Did you see that bird

4. Can he eat that big hamburger

5. A bird flew into the room

6. Is your brother here

7. She did not see her friend

C   Write **N** above each noun.
Write **P** above each pronoun.
Write **V** above each verb.

1. She stood next to him.

2. That girl gave him a book.

3. James saw her through that window.

4. Our cat played with them.

5. They were on top of it.

TEST 4

Test Score [ ]

A Write **N** above each noun.
Write **P** above each pronoun.
Write **V** above each verb.

1. That new <u>boy</u> <u>sat</u> next to <u>him</u>.

2. <u>Linda</u> and her friend <u>fixed</u> <u>it</u>.

3. <u>She</u> <u>took</u> <u>them</u> to the park.

4. Six <u>cows</u> <u>walked</u> behind <u>her</u>.

B Rewrite each sentence so it begins with the part that tells when.

1. She fixed her car in the morning.

_____

_____

2. He went to sleep after he brushed his teeth.

_____

_____

3. The baby woke up when the bell rang.

_____

_____

4. Nobody talked during the movie.

_____

_____

C The number after each item tells how many mistakes are in the item. Fix up the mistakes.

1. Marias dog chased two cats up a tree (2)

2. The babies fell asleep on anns bed. (2)

3. Mr. adams said "I liked that book. (3)

4. Ann met Lindas brother he was very tall. (3)

5. He said my team won the game. (4)

D For each picture, write the sentences that tell the exact words the person said.

1.	
2.	

A   Put commas in the sentences that begin with the part that tells when.

1. A cat jumped up when the alarm clock rang.

2. When we got home the dog started barking.

3. In the morning we ate breakfast.

4. While the baby slept we talked quietly.

5. Her brother was happy when he got the letter.

6. They finished the job just before midnight.

7. Before they made lunch the cooks washed their hands.

B   For each sentence, fill in the blank with the word **asked** or the word **said.** Then make the correct ending mark.

1. The girl _____, "Will you go with us "

2. The girl _____, "I want to go with you "

3. My friend _____, "I love baseball "

4. My friend _____, "Do you like baseball "

5. Ken _____, "Is it snowing "

6. Ken _____, "The snow is two feet deep "

C   Write **N** in front of each noun.

1. _____ girl

2. _____ men

3. _____ they

4. _____ us

5. _____ yellow

6. _____ phone

7. _____ happy

8. _____ me

9. _____ mud

A Write **N** above each noun.
Write **P** above each pronoun.
Write **V** above each verb.

1. They were on top of it.

2. A big dog followed them up the hill.

3. She gave him the ball.

4. Jerry was next to her.

B Write **N** in front of each noun.

1. _____ pen   5. _____ song   9. _____ clouds

2. _____ us   6. _____ them   10. _____ school

3. _____ flag   7. _____ her   11. _____ puppies

4. _____ under   8. _____ found   12. _____ party

C For each sentence, fill in the blank with the word **asked** or the word **said.** Then make the correct ending mark.

1. He _____, "Why are you so sad "

2. She _____, "He has my book "

3. His friend _____, "Where is the game "

4. My sister _____, "Can we have a cookie "

A

1. She bought a new car.

2. They went to a crowded beach.

3. Sam cooked dinner for them.

4. My truck ran over it.

B For each sentence, fill in the blank with the word **asked** or the word **said.** Then make the correct ending mark.

1. He _____, "Is your brother home "

2. He _____, "We had a good time "

3. She _____, "My friend went home "

4. She _____, "Where is the dog "

C Copy the paragraph. Change three sentences so they begin with the part that tells when.

Tom got up early in the morning. He ate breakfast after he put on warm

clothes. Carol and her mother came over to Tom's house at 9 o'clock. They

took Tom to a mountain. It was covered with snow. Tom and Carol threw

snowballs when they got to the mountain top.

Lesson 44

A Punctuate the sentences that tell the exact words a person said. Put in the missing commas, quote marks and capital letters.

Jerry called Tom on the phone. Jerry asked Tom can you go to the movies?

Tom asked his mother can I go to the movies?

His mother said you can go when you finish your homework.

Tom finished his homework quickly. Tom's mom took Jerry and Tom to the movies later that day.

B Write **N** above each noun.
Write **P** above each pronoun.
Write **V** above each verb.

1. The <u>wind</u> <u>blew</u> <u>water</u> at <u>them</u>.

2. My <u>brother</u> <u>put</u> <u>salt</u> on <u>it</u>.

3. <u>She</u> <u>wanted</u> a new <u>bike</u> last <u>summer</u>.

4. That old <u>man</u> <u>sold</u> <u>it</u> to <u>me</u>.

C

1. At midnight. The dog began to bark. (2)

2. The streets flooded, during the rain storm (2)

3. She bought a book. Before the store closed. (2)

4. While the wind blew. Everybody stayed inside Toms house. (3)

5. Ann fell asleep while toms dad sang. (2)

6. Two old trees fell down, last night. (1)

7. Before Anns dad made breakfast we washed our hands. (2)

A Write **N** above each noun.
Write **P** above each pronoun.
Write **V** above each verb.

1. He threw it at the wall.

2. Tim and Donna were mad at them.

3. The dogs and cats ran after me.

4. Her arm had a bug on it.

B Fix up any mistakes in each item.

1. When alice got to school. Nobody was there. (3)

2. Jerry asked his mother can I stay home?" (3)

3. Tom asked his sister where is my shirt (5)

4. My sister wasn't home. She went to alices house. (2)

5. As mr. jordan left. The children waved to him. (4)

6. Bill cleaned his room, before he ate breakfast (2)

A

Write **N** above each noun.
Write **P** above each pronoun.
Write **V** above each verb.

1. A <u>girl</u> and her <u>dog</u> <u>chased</u> <u>it</u> around the park.

2. <u>He</u> <u>was</u> between a little <u>desk</u> and a big <u>table</u>.

3. Yesterday morning, <u>she</u> <u>ate</u> <u>eggs</u> and toast for <u>breakfast</u>.

4. In the <u>morning</u>, <u>they</u> <u>took</u> him to see <u>me</u>.

B

A.　　　　　B.　　　　　C.　　　　　D.

1. The boy was tall. _____

2. The boy was tall. He wore shorts. _____

3. The boy was tall. He wore shorts. He held a bat. _____

A

1. Ted and <u>Hilda</u> <u>were</u> on the <u>bank</u> of a <u>stream</u>.

2. When the <u>sun</u> came up, Ginger and <u>Tom</u> <u>walked</u> to the <u>barn</u>.

3. Before <u>school</u>, the little <u>boy</u> <u>looked</u> for <u>them</u>.

4. <u>She</u> <u>felt</u> tired after the <u>party</u>.

B | **Rule:** If you remove the word **and,** you must replace it with a comma.

1. Ann had fun swimming <u>and</u> playing ball and digging in the sand.

2. Girls <u>and</u> boys <u>and</u> dogs and cats slid down the hill.

3. James read a book and wrote two letters and called his uncle and cleaned his room.

4. A cat and a dog and a pig and a horse ran into the barn.

C

   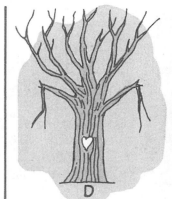

A   B   C   D

1. The tree was small. _____

2. The tree was small. It had broken branches. _____

3. The tree was small. It had broken branches. It had a heart carved on it.

A

1. A <u>dog</u> and a <u>cat</u> <u>were</u> next to <u>her</u>.

2. After the <u>rain</u> <u>stopped</u>, <u>they</u> went to his <u>house</u>.

3. <u>She</u> <u>put</u> <u>apples</u> and <u>oranges</u> in her bag.

4. Yesterday <u>morning</u>, their <u>mother</u> <u>drove</u> <u>them</u> to school.

B

- If there are two **ands,** cross out the first **and.** Replace it with a comma.
- If there is only one **and,** leave it.

1. Tom ate chicken and peas and carrots.

2. Jane jumped rope and climbed on the bars and walked on her hands.

3. Jerry jumped up and ran to the door.

4. A book and a pencil and a cup fell off the table.

5. Alice opened the door and got into the car and drove to work.

6. James and his sister went home.

7. Jane and Tom and Bill ate lunch under the tree.

C

1. The house had two trees next to it. It had broken windows. _____

2. The house had two trees next to it. It had broken windows. It had a

chimney. _____

3. The house had two trees next to it. _____

Lesson
49

A
- If there are two **ands,** cross out the first **and.** Replace it with a comma.
- If there is only one **and,** leave it.

1. Jerry got into the car and turned on the engine and drove home.

2. Mary and Jim and Tom were sick yesterday.

3. James ate a piece of bread and drank a glass of milk.

4. Bill wore black shoes and a red shirt and brown pants.

5. A cat and a dog and a pig lived in the barn.

6. My mother and my little sister walked to the store.

7. Walter washed the windows and made his bed and swept the floor.

B   Fix up any mistakes in each item.

1. Bill asked his mother when will we eat dinner (5)

2. When the dog barked at a cat. The baby woke up. (2)

3. Tom brushed his teeth, after he washed his face (2)

4. Abdul said, "I am hungry. I want an apple (2)

5. The boys cleaned their teachers desk. (1)

6. Where is mr. suzuki (3)

TEST 5

 A   Write **N** above each noun.
Write **P** above each pronoun.
Write **V** above each verb.

1. My sister found them in her coat.

2. In the morning, he wrote a letter.

3. Yesterday afternoon, they saw a movie about Texas.

4. She walked in the street with her dog.

B   For each sentence, circle the subject and underline the whole predicate.

1. My sister and I went home on the bus.

2. After the sun went down, the sky became cloudy.

3. While the baby slept, everybody whispered.

4. Those birds will fly away when they finish eating.

5. In the evening, James read a book.

C For each sentence, fill in the blank with the word **asked** or the word **said.** Then make the correct ending mark.

1. James _____, "Can you help me "

2. They _____, "We won the game "

3. She _____, "My dog's name is Rover "

4. He _____, "What is your dog's name "

D Put a comma in each sentence that begins with the part that tells when.

1. While the wind blew everybody stayed inside.

2. My sister got home before I did.

3. After the rain stopped my friends and I walked home.

4. As she walked home Julie listened to the music.

5. An old tree fell down during the storm.

6. Before our dad made breakfast we cleaned our room.

7. All the cars stopped when the light turned red.

Lesson 51

 A Complete each sentence with the verb **was** or the verb **were.**

1. Those girls _____ happy.

2. Girls and boys _____ hungry.

3. A baby _____ sleepy.

4. Five dogs _____ chasing a cat.

5. Those three books _____ new.

6. My mother _____ next to the car.

7. He _____ at the park.

8. They _____ late for school.

B

1. <u>She</u> <u>had</u> more <u>stickers</u> than James had.

2. Yesterday <u>afternoon</u>, <u>they</u> <u>cleaned</u> their <u>room</u>.

3. When the <u>sun</u> came up, <u>Alice</u> <u>called</u> <u>him</u>.

4. My <u>sister</u> <u>gave</u> <u>me</u> a new shirt.

C Fix up the sentences that have too many **ands.**

1. They bought three apples and six oranges.

2. His sister bought five apples and two oranges and three carrots.

3. Raymond and Ned talked quietly.

4. Alice and Julio and Clark talked quietly.

5. We cleaned our room and ate dinner and did our homework before we went to sleep.

A Complete each sentence with the verb **was** or the verb **were.**

1. My father _____ sick.

2. Her older brothers _____ behind the car.

3. They _____ eating dinner.

4. Two horses _____ in the barn.

5. I _____ walking my dog.

6. Their dad _____ eating lunch.

7. My mother and father _____ happy.

B

1. Last <u>winter</u>, <u>they</u> <u>went</u> to see their <u>grandmother</u>.

2. <u>It</u> <u>was</u> next to the big <u>bottle</u>.

3. After <u>they</u> ate, <u>she</u> <u>played</u> with the <u>baby</u>.

4. <u>Linda</u> and <u>James</u> <u>sat</u> near <u>me</u>.

C Use your lined paper. Rewrite each sentence so the word **and** appears only once.

1. The boy ran and slipped on the ice and fell down.

2. John and Mary and Jim went jogging.

3. They were tired and thirsty and hungry.

A Complete each sentence with the verb **was** or the verb **were.**

1. Jenny and John _____ reading.

2. That pencil _____ sharp.

3. Five fish _____ swimming in the tank.

4. Terry _____ fishing from the boat.

5. An old woman _____ tired.

6. They _____ playing football.

B Fix up any mistakes in each item.

1. Alice asked, "where is my car (3)

2. After mr. adams ate. he went home. (3)

3. James asked his mother can I go out to play?" (3)

4. Alice sat down, when she finished the race. (1)

5. Two birds flew over anns head (3)

A Complete each sentence with the verb **was** or the verb **were**.

1. You _____ right.

2. You _____ late yesterday.

3. She _____ sad.

4. You _____ not home yesterday.

5. He _____ late.

6. They _____ sick.

7. His dog _____ friendly.

8. You _____ hiding.

B

1. Write a description about picture 1. Tell where the women were and what they were doing.

2. Write a description about picture 2. Tell where the women were and what they were doing.

A

1. Suddenly, a big <u>wind</u> <u>knocked</u> <u>him</u> off the <u>chair</u>.

2. He <u>put</u> a <u>cow</u> and a <u>pig</u> in the old red <u>barn</u>.

3. After <u>lunch</u>, my <u>mother</u> took <u>me</u> to the swimming <u>pool</u>.

4. A <u>snowball</u> <u>landed</u> next to <u>her</u>.

B   For each noun, write **day, month** or **name.**

1. Jay Turner _____

2. October _____

3. Wednesday _____

4. Friday _____

5. David _____

6. December _____

 C

1. Make up a sentence that tells who **went into the store.**
2. Make up a sentence that tells which animals **stood on a diving board.**
3. Make up a sentence that tells the things **the woman juggled.**

A

Pronouns	Names	Pronouns
	Sue and Alice	
I •	Mrs. Jones	• we
	Tom and Jill	
me •	Sam	• us
	Mary	
	Ted, Ned and Fred	

B

1. After the <u>rain</u> stopped, <u>we</u> <u>walked</u> to <u>school</u>.

2. Last night, <u>I</u> <u>helped</u> <u>him</u> do his <u>homework</u>.

3. The <u>airplane</u> <u>took</u> <u>her</u> to <u>Texas</u>.

4. <u>She</u> <u>taught</u> <u>me</u> how to fix <u>bikes</u>.

A

Pronouns	Names	Pronouns
	Mr. Alvarez	
I •	Alice and Jane	• we
	Bryan, Tim and Robin	
me •	Jason	• us
	Chris and James	
	Debbie	

B Fix up the mistakes in each item.

1. Tom and I was both born on the first wednesday in december. (3)

2. Janes hand got dirty, when she planted trees (3)

3. Ann visited her grandmother every monday night in april and may. (3)

4. Cats and dogs was running in Toms yard. (2)

5. Alex and i were talking to cora. (2)

6. Kay asked her dad can i stay up late? (5)

7. When mr. adams got home on Thursday. He read the newspaper. (4)

A

1. At last, my <u>brother</u> and <u>I</u> <u>finished</u> our <u>homework</u>.

2. Yesterday, <u>we</u> <u>helped</u> <u>Mary</u> fix her <u>car</u>.

3. <u>Alice</u> and her <u>sister</u> <u>were</u> not with <u>me</u>.

4. Her <u>car</u> <u>had</u> a racing <u>stripe</u>.

B   Fix up the mistakes in each item.

1. Mr. Adams and mrs. sanchez was sick on wednesday. (4)

2. Jill asked Tom can i help you?" (4)

3. When my mom walked into the room. My baby sister smiled. (2)

4. Where did you put Jills coat (2)

5. You was born in february. (2)

6. She asked was he born in september or october?" (5)

Lesson
60

A

1. After the <u>rain</u> stopped, Alice and <u>I</u> <u>walked</u> home.

2. <u>We</u> <u>played</u> <u>basketball</u> with a tall <u>man</u>.

3. My <u>friend</u> <u>was</u> next to <u>me</u>.

4. After we <u>ate</u> lunch, <u>Bob</u> showed <u>us</u> how to fly <u>kites</u>.

B

1. Make up a sentence that tells who chased the squirrel.
2. Make up a sentence that tells what Raymond was holding.

1. Last night, <u>we</u> <u>ate</u> dinner in a <u>restaurant</u>.

2. Her big <u>sister</u> <u>was</u> not with <u>them</u>.

3. <u>I</u> <u>called</u> <u>her</u> this <u>morning</u>.

4. When the <u>rain</u> stopped, Liz and <u>Alex</u> <u>walked</u> home.

B

Rule: Any word that comes before the noun in the subject is an adjective.

           N
1. A little puppy is barking.
           N
2. Nine boys ate lunch.
                 N
3. A beautiful red kite flew in the air.

C

For each sentence, circle the subject.
- Write **N** above the noun in the subject.
- Write **A** above each adjective in the subject.

1. An old tree grew next to the house.

2. That farmer had big hands.

3. Six little black cats ran in front of me.

4. Small clouds moved across the sky.

5. Those happy boys cheered loudly.

6. The dog was hungry.

          Lesson 61

D Fix up the four unclear words in this passage.

One day, Tom and his dog went to the park with a Frisbee. The dog loved to play with the Frisbee and wagged its tail as they went to the park. As Tom and his dog played, they came out of the woods to watch.

Tom was pretending he was a star baseball player. He threw the Frisbee as hard as he could. It went over the dog's head and landed in the field. Tom and his dog ran after the Frisbee. It grabbed the Frisbee.

As the dog barked at the bear cubs, she came out from behind the trees. When Tom saw the mother bear, he grabbed it and climbed up a tree.

Lesson 62

A Fix up the four unclear words.

Kevin

Ramon

Ramon and Kevin worked at a rodeo. Kevin was a cowboy who rode

bulls. He was a rodeo clown who helped cowboys.

One day, he tried to ride a fierce bull. He held on tightly as the bull jumped

up and down. Suddenly, the bull turned sharply and threw Kevin to the ground.

As Kevin sat on the ground holding his leg, he ran into the rodeo arena holding

it over his head. Ramon put the barrel down on the ground and began to yell

at the bull. The bull turned and ran toward the barrel. While Ramon helped

Kevin walk away, the bull hit the barrel with its horns. Ramon had once again

helped a cowboy who was in danger.

A Fix up the three unclear words in this passage.

Raymond   beehive   the pond

Raymond loved to throw rocks. While Raymond was walking through

the woods one day, he picked up some rocks and started throwing them at a

tree. One rock missed the tree and hit it. They were very mad. They flew out of

the hive and headed straight toward Raymond. He ran away as quickly as he

could. Just before the bees reached Raymond, he jumped into it. He stayed in

the pond until the bees returned to their nest.

A

1. His brother bought a new hat.

2. My sister baked a yellow cake.

3. Five red ants climbed the kitchen wall.

4. An old red cup fell off the big table.

B   Fix up the mistakes in each sentence.

1. Jerry asked, "can Raymond and i go to the movies (4)

2. My dads hand is twice as big as Jerrys hand. (2)

3. When the baby fell asleep. Everybody was happy. (2)

4. Alice Chuck and ellen ate lunch at Ellens house. (3)

5. December january and february was cold months. (4)

6. Alice was very tired, when she got home on monday. (2)

- Write **N** above each noun.
- Write **A** above each adjective.

1. One man held a big net.

2. Her children bought ten cookies.

3. The gray squirrel climbed a tall tree.

4. Two children washed their little dog.

B

Cross out the letters of the sentences that are **not** relevant to the question.

> **How is wood used?**

ⓐ Wood is used for building things. ⓑ Wood is also used for fuel. ⓒ Some houses have walls that are made of wood. ⓓ Other houses are made of brick. ⓔ The floors of many houses are made of wood. ⓕ Some houses have floors made of concrete. ⓖ Concrete floors may crack when the house gets old. ⓗ Some window frames are made of wood. ⓘ Fine tables and chairs are made of wood. ⓙ Other chairs are made of metal or plastic.

C Fix up the three unclear words in this passage.

Early one morning, Tina drove her car to the garage where Robert, Sam

and Jane worked. After Tina parked her car in front of the gas pumps, he

walked to the back of the car and opened the gas tank cover. As Robert put

gas in the car, he cleaned the front windows. She bent down and took a tire off

a car while the men worked on Tina's car.

A Write adjectives that make each subject complete.

1. _____ rabbit

2. _____ men

3. _____ cup

4. _____ monster

B

1. Suddenly, <u>he</u> <u>jumped</u> out of <u>bed</u>.

2. Nine <u>men</u> <u>helped</u> <u>me</u> fix my <u>car</u>.

3. <u>Dan</u> and his <u>sister</u> <u>were</u> with <u>us</u>.

4. After <u>we</u> <u>ate</u>, my <u>mother</u> was tired.

C The writer forgot to punctuate the sentences that tell the exact words somebody said. Fix up those sentences.

	James did not do his homework last night. He said my teacher won't care. She likes me. James was wrong. His teacher did care. She said you will stay in from recess to finish your work. James was not happy during recess. He said tonight I will finish my homework before I watch TV I don't like missing recess.

A Capitalize all parts of any item that names one person or one place.

1. that boy

2. tom

3. mrs. robert brown

4. my teacher

5. lincoln street

6. a repair shop

7. johnson repair shop

8. chicago, illinois

9. mississippi river

10. my store

11. jolly time toy store

12. that river

 B Cross out the letters of the sentences that are **not** relevant to the question.

| **What did Bob and Sally do when they saw a burning house?** |

ⓐ Bob and Sally ran into the house when they saw smoke coming from the house. ⓑ While Bob filled a pail with water, Sally grabbed the fire extinguisher. ⓒ Bob and Sally worked in the same factory. ⓓ They saw that a chair and a table were on fire. ⓔ Bob threw water on the chair while Sally squirted the fire extinguisher on the table. ⓕ That night, Bob and Sally watched television.

 C
- Write **N** above each noun.
- Write **A** above each adjective.

1. Three sad clowns rode a tiny bicycle.

2. Kathy is sleeping on the couch.

3. A striped kite hit the tree.

4. A cow ate grass.

Lesson 68

A Capitalize all parts of any item that names one person or one place.

1. uncle jake

2. the street

3. san francisco

4. kennedy high school

5. our uncle

6. ace toy factory

7. united states

8. the mail carrier

9. pacific ocean

10. a big country

11. japan

12. adams street

B
- Write **N** above each noun.
- Write **A** above each adjective.

1. His bear juggled three balls.

2. A sick boy sat in a wheelchair.

3. Al ate two apples.

4. That woman held a small red purse.

5. Three people fixed that old red car.

C Put the missing comma in each sentence that begins with a part that tells when.

As Wendy drove home from work she thought of the banana pie that was in the refrigerator. Wendy was very hungry because she had not eaten lunch. After she parked her car she ran into the kitchen and opened the refrigerator. Wendy could not believe her eyes. The refrigerator was empty. The banana pie was gone. Everything was gone. While Wendy was looking at the empty refrigerator her brother walked into the kitchen. He looked nervous. After a few seconds he walked up to his sister and said, "I'm sorry. I had some friends over for lunch and we ate all the food. Wait here. I'll be right back." Wendy sat down and waited. After a few minutes her brother walked into the kitchen. He was carrying a bag filled with groceries. While Wendy took a nap her brother cooked dinner. The dessert was a huge banana pie.

Lesson 69

 A Capitalize all parts of any item that names one person or one place.

1. ruth garcia

2. a doctor

3. a big building

4. fairview hospital

5. don's supermarket

6. dr. brown

7. that avenue

8. salt lake city

9. mr. jordan

10. his street

11. florida

12. spring avenue

 B

1. <u>Seven</u> <u>men</u> <u>went</u> to <u>a</u> <u>big</u> <u>party</u>.

2. <u>Two</u> <u>little</u> <u>children</u> <u>stood</u> in <u>deep</u> <u>snow</u>.

3. <u>James</u> <u>was</u> <u>wearing</u> <u>striped</u> <u>shorts</u>.

4. <u>An</u> <u>old</u> <u>woman</u> <u>gave</u> me <u>a</u> <u>dollar</u>.

C The writer forgot to punctuate the sentences that tell the exact words somebody said. Fix up those sentences.

David walked up to his sister. He said I have a problem. My bike won't work.

She said I will help you fix it. They worked for two hours. After they finished, the bike worked as well as ever.

David said Thanks a lot. I really am happy that you are my sister.

TEST 7

Lesson 70

A Write **V** above each verb.
Write **N** above each noun.
Write **A** above each adjective.

1. Six new cars went up the steep hill.

2. A strong wind knocked over an old fence.

B Fix up each sentence so it is punctuated correctly.

1. Alice had a dog a cat and a bird. (1)

2. Mr. James Mrs. James and their son ate breakfast. (1)

3. We bought apples oranges and pears at the store. (1)

C Capitalize all parts of any item that names one person or one place.

1. a big store   4. california   7. that river

2. united states   5. washington avenue   8. ace toy store

3. dr. mitchell   6. her house

D Fill in each blank with the verb **was** or **were.**

1. They _____ not home.

2. Jim's cat _____ sitting on the fence.

3. Anna and her mother _____ at the store.

4. You _____ right.

5. An old man _____ fishing.

6. You _____ not home last night.

A   For each item, write the sentence that answers the question.

1. Question: What are cheetahs?
   Answer: The fastest land animals.

2. Question: Where do cheetahs live?
   Answer: In Africa.

3. Question: When do cheetahs hunt?
   Answer: During the day.

4. Question: How fast do cheetahs run?
   Answer: Over 60 miles an hour.

B

1. Five lions were in the cage.

2. A small airplane is landing now.

3. Steve was swimming in cold water.

4. The red ball bounced into a busy street.

C Put the missing comma in each sentence that begins with a part that tells when.

Mr. Ross took his family out for dinner at a fancy restaurant. They had a very expensive meal. After they finished the meal, the waiter brought them the bill. Mr. Ross reached into his pocket for his wallet. As he reached into his pocket, he realized that he had left his wallet at home. He told the waiter about his problem. The waiter told the boss that Mr. Ross could not pay the bill. When the boss heard about the problem, she was not happy. The boss and Mr. Ross talked and came up with a solution to the problem. While his family went home to look for the wallet, Mr. Ross had to begin washing dishes. Mr. Ross put on an apron and began to wash the dishes. By the time his family came back with his wallet, Mr. Ross had washed all the dishes in the restaurant.

A   For each item, write the sentence that answers the question.

1. Question: Where do the largest elephants live?
   Answer: In Africa.

2. Question: How long do some elephants live?
   Answer: More than 50 years.

3. Question: How much do some elephants weigh?
   Answer: Up to six tons.

B

1. When <u>the</u> <u>bell</u> rang, <u>we</u> <u>went</u> to <u>our</u> <u>classroom</u>.

2. <u>Linda</u> <u>stood</u> in front of <u>a</u> <u>large</u> <u>desk</u>.

3. <u>That</u> <u>tiny</u> <u>black</u> <u>fly</u> <u>flew</u> into <u>my</u> <u>cup</u>.

4. During <u>the</u> <u>night</u>, <u>a</u> <u>strong</u> <u>wind</u> <u>blew</u>.

A   For each item, write the sentence that answers the question.

1. Question: Where do you find skunks?
   Answer: In North America.

2. Question: Why do skunks make a terrible smell?
   Answer: To defend themselves.

3. Question: When do skunks usually sleep?
   Answer: During the daytime.

4. Question: How do skunks show that they are angry?
   Answer: By raising their tails.

B

1. During the big storm, we went inside an old house.

2. He saw many black ants on the kitchen table.

3. Two old men helped her.

4. His truck moved slowly up a steep hill.

5. After the meeting, she went to the store.

A

1. <u>I</u> <u>found</u> <u>four</u> <u>red</u> <u>marbles</u> under <u>that</u> <u>old</u> <u>rug</u>.

2. <u>Every</u> <u>day</u>, <u>we</u> <u>buy</u> <u>milk</u> at <u>the</u> <u>store</u>.

3. <u>An</u> <u>airplane</u> <u>flew</u> over <u>a</u> <u>big</u> <u>white</u> <u>cloud</u>.

4. <u>A</u> <u>bright</u> <u>light</u> <u>came</u> from <u>the</u> <u>third</u> <u>floor</u>.

B

1. The mississippi river is the longest river in the united states. (4)

2. Texas alaska and california are the biggest states. (3)

3. Is los angeles bigger than san francisco? (4)

4. We lived on baldwin street until last september. (3)

5. After she brushed her teeth. She went to bed. (2)

6. My favorite cities are new york dallas and miami. (5)

7. Ann asked mr. james Where can i buy that book (7)

A

1. Before the rain stopped.

_____

2. Stood on top of the table.

_____

3. She caught a bug.

_____

4. Mary sat down.

_____

5. Mary, Tom and their dog.

_____

6. After the show.

_____

B

1. After <u>the</u> <u>storm</u>, <u>we</u> <u>had</u> <u>a</u> <u>fish</u> in <u>our</u> <u>basement</u>.

2. <u>His</u> <u>mother</u> <u>told</u> <u>us</u> <u>a</u> <u>funny</u> <u>story</u>.

3. In <u>my</u> <u>dream</u>, <u>five</u> <u>tigers</u> <u>were</u> <u>chasing</u> <u>me</u>.

4. <u>Tom</u> and <u>Fran</u> <u>ran</u> over <u>that</u> <u>hill</u>.

1. After we finished eating.

   _____

2. He opened it.

   _____

3. A shirt, blue jeans and shoes.

   _____

4. Before the snow stopped.

   _____

5. She jumped up.

   _____

B Write a good title sentence for each passage.

Passage 1

   Laurie put on her swimming suit. She jumped into the pool. She swam across the pool three times. Then she got out of the pool and dried off.

   _____

Passage 2

   Ted made his bed. He picked up his dirty clothes from the bedroom floor. He put things in his closet. He swept the floor of his room. Then he cleaned the windows in his room.

   _____

C   Fix up the four unclear words in this passage.

James and Mike looked at the robot they had just built. The robot was standing in the corner of the room holding a fishbowl over its head. It ran away from the robot while the boys stood behind a big cardboard box.

"This is a disaster," he said.

"I told you to be careful when you put the wires together," he said.

The robot had already knocked over a lamp and broken a window. The dog was terrified. It said, "I must destroy. I must destroy."

       Lesson 76   **119**

Lesson 77

A Write a good title sentence for each passage.

Passage 1

Kurt grabbed his dog and took it into the bathroom. He filled the bathtub with water. He put the dog in the tub. He rubbed soap on the dog. He rinsed off the dog.

_____

Passage 2

Brad took a can of cat food from the shelf. He opened the can. He put the cat food in a small dish. Then he put the dish on the floor. His cat ate all the food.

_____

B For each sentence, circle the subject and underline the predicate.
- Write **N** above each underlined noun.
- Write **A** above each underlined adjective.
- Write **V** above each underlined verb.
- Write **P** above each underlined pronoun.

1. Fran and Ray ran to the beach.

2. In the evening, I saw big spiders on our front steps.

3. That old car runs like a new car.

4. He slipped on the icy stairs.

A Write a good title sentence for each passage.

Passage 1

Steve took out some paper and a pen. He wrote on the paper. He put the paper in an envelope. He wrote his grandmother's name and address on the envelope. He put a stamp on the envelope.

_____

Passage 2

Melody put some paper in the fireplace. She put wood on top of the paper. She lit a match and held it under the paper. When the paper and wood started to burn, Melody closed the screen in front of the fireplace.

_____

1. The empire state building is in new york. (5)

2. Robert fed the dog washed the dishes and cleaned his room before

   lunch. (1)

3. Is mexico larger than canada (3)

4. Jill asked, "Where is Dr. Lees office? (2)

5. I bought apples oranges and pears at the store. (1)

6. December january and february are the coldest months of the year. (3)

7. Yokos sister lives on washington street. (3)

8. Tom and his sister was in the park. (1)

A

1. Before we went to sleep.

_____

2. She helped him.

_____

3. When they got home.

_____

4. A truck, a car and a motorcycle.

_____

5. He stopped talking.

_____

B For each sentence, circle the subject and underline the predicate.
• Write **N** above each underlined noun.
• Write **A** above each underlined adjective.
• Write **V** above each underlined verb.
• Write **P** above each underlined pronoun.

1. A large red truck stopped in front of them.

2. After school, six boys and two girls played in the gym.

3. She helped him fix the flat tire on his new bike.

TEST 8

Test Score

Lesson
80

A

1. In <u>the</u> <u>morning</u>, <u>my</u> <u>older</u> sister fixed breakfast for <u>our</u> <u>family</u>.

2. <u>That</u> <u>old</u> <u>car</u> <u>stopped</u> in front of <u>a</u> <u>large</u> <u>building</u>.

3. <u>She</u> <u>was</u> <u>smiling</u> when <u>they</u> <u>went</u> out <u>the</u> <u>back</u> <u>door</u>.

4. <u>Two</u> <u>mean</u> <u>dogs</u> <u>were</u> <u>running</u> after <u>a</u> <u>yellow</u> <u>cat</u>.

B

1. When she got home. everybody was sleeping. (1)

2. I live on madison avenue. (2)

3. The mississippi river is the longest river in the united states. (4)

4. Renee asked Alfred, "Have you seen my brother? He has my pen. (1)

5. Bills favorite team is the san francisco giants. (4)

6. June july and august are the warmest months. (3)

7. Does dr. spangler have an office on washington street (5)

A Fix up the five unclear words in this passage.

Just after the school bell rang, a strange thing happened. It walked into the classroom on its hind legs. The students couldn't believe their eyes. She was making marks on a piece of paper and didn't see the strange animal. The alligator walked toward a seat next to a girl named Ann. "Why is everybody looking at the door?" she asked.

"The new student has arrived," he said.

"Can the new student sit next to me?" she asked. She clapped her hands as she thought about the strange things that might happen that day.

Lesson 81

A   Use Reading Textbook B to answer these questions.

1. What part of your textbook shows a list of the selections in the book,

   starting with page 1? _____

2. What is the title of the selection for lesson 134?

   _____

3. On what page does the selection for lesson 134 begin? _____

4. What is the title of the selection for lesson 99? _____

5. On what page does that selection begin? _____

B

1. Write the date for the fifth day of August in the year 1968.

   _____

2. Write the date for the third day of June in the year 2001.

   _____

3. Write the date for the eleventh day of March in the year 1792.

   _____

4. Write the date for the eighth day of July in the year 1812.

   _____

5. Write the date for the nineteenth day of November in the year 1947.

   _____

A Use the table of contents in Reading Textbook B to answer these questions.

1. How many selections are listed for lesson 79? _____

2. What's the title of the information passage? _____

3. What's the title of the story for lesson 79? _____

4. On what page does the story for lesson 79 begin? _____

5. What's the title for the selection that begins on page 138?

_____

B

1. Write the date for the 21st day of May in the year 1886.

_____

2. Write the date for the seventeenth day of September in the year 2010.

_____

3. Write the date for the tenth day of January in the year 1935.

_____

4. Write the date for the 23rd day of March in the year 1722.

_____

C

| great | carrot | top | horse | right |
| visit | elephant | north | jail | millions |

Ⓐ Use the table of contents in Reading Textbook B to answer these questions.

1. How many selections are listed for lesson 126? _____

2. What's the page number for the first selection in lesson 126? _____

3. What's the page number for the second selection in lesson 126? _____

4. What's the title of the second selection? _____

Ⓑ

1. Greenville Iowa _____

2. Street number: 45
   Street name: Vine Street
   City name: Greenville
   State name: Iowa
   Write the address with commas.

   _____

3. Street number: 7
   Street name: Old Goat Road
   City name: Chico
   State name: California
   Write the address with commas.

   _____

Ⓒ

| length | bedroom | globe | yellow | desk |
| raise | should | forest | umbrella | whole |

Lesson 85

A

1. arrange _____

2. join _____

3. appear _____

4. charge _____

B Write **jump** or **jumps** in each sentence. Write **one** or **more than one** after each sentence.

1. The girl _____.   _____

2. You and I _____.   _____

3. Cats and dogs _____.   _____

4. Those frogs _____.   _____

5. A man _____.   _____

6. Mark and Henry _____.   _____

C Use the words below to make an alphabetical list.

higher   unless

tongue   funny

ocean   question

yourself   normal

insect   knocked

A Write **run** or **runs** in each sentence. Write **one** or **more than one** after each sentence.

1. This woman _____. _____

2. Boys and girls _____. _____

3. She _____. _____

4. Her pals _____. _____

5. Her pal _____. _____

6. Two men _____. _____

B

1	**2**	**3**
1. approve	_____	_____
2. arrange	_____	_____
3. order	_____	_____
4. join	_____	_____
5. connect	_____	_____

C Use the words below to make an alphabetical list.

kitten   dance
officer   lifeboat
argued   half

A Use the table of contents in Reading Textbook B to answer these questions.

1. What's the lesson number for the selection that begins on page 303? _____

2. What's the title of the selection that begins on page 303?

    _____

3. What's the lesson number for the selection that begins on page 91? _____

4. What's the title of the selection that begins on page 91?

    _____

B   1   2   3

1. join   _____   _____

2. order   _____   _____

3. charge   _____   _____

4. connect   _____   _____

5. continue   _____   _____

C Write **hop** or **hops** in each sentence. Write **one** or **more than one** after each sentence.

1. Joan and Barry _____ over logs.   _____

2. She _____ over logs.   _____

3. They _____ over logs.   _____

4. This thin man _____ over logs.   _____

A Write **sing** or **sings** in each sentence. Write **one** or **more than one** after each sentence.

1. His dad _____ well.   _____

2. His dad and mom _____ well.   _____

3. Those ten kids _____ well.   _____

4. Her older brothers _____ well.   _____

A Write **talk** or **talks** in each sentence. Write **one** or **more than one** after each sentence.

1. She _____ fast.   _____

2. That man _____ fast.   _____

3. Alvin and his brother _____ fast.   _____

4. Six parrots _____ fast.   _____

A

coat	mirror	1. _____
climb	myna	2. _____
canned	metal	3. _____
curly	money	4. _____
crazy	machine	5. _____

B   Write the word for each description.

1. What word means **without effort?** _____

2. What word means **without a home?** _____

3. What word means **to connect again?** _____

4. What word means **the opposite of connect?** _____

5. What word means **not zipped?** _____

6. What word means **without a hat?** _____

A Write the first page of Reading Textbook B that tells about each topic.

1. blizzard _____

2. lungs _____

3. universe _____

4. Jupiter _____

B Underline the second letter in each word. Then write the words in alphabetical order.

squirrel

steady

scale

solid

smelly

shelves

1. _____

2. _____

3. _____

4. _____

5. _____

6. _____

C Write **run** or **runs** in each sentence. Write **one** or **more than one** after each sentence.

1. Those cars _____ on batteries. _____

2. That river _____ to the sea. _____

3. Dogs _____ faster than people. _____

4. This man _____ every day. _____

D   Write the word for each description.

1. What word means **full of thought?**   _____

2. What word means **the opposite of charged?**   _____

3. What word means **without roads?**   _____

4. What word means **to think again?**   _____

5. What word means **without care?**   _____

6. What word means **full of care?**   _____

A   Use Reading Textbook B to answer these questions.

1. You want to find the first page in the Reading Textbook that tells about computers. On what page does that topic begin? _____

2. Write the first word on that page. _____

3. What is the last page on which the topic **computer** appears? _____

4. Write the last word on that page. _____

5. You want to find the first page in the textbook that tells about **elephants.** On what page does that topic begin? _____

6. Write the first word on that page. _____

7. What is the last page on which the topic **elephant** appears? _____

8. Write the last word on that page. _____

B   Write **like** or **likes** in each sentence. Write **one** or **more than one** after each sentence.

1. His dad _____ golf.   _____

2. Her parents _____ to dance.   _____

3. Kittens _____ milk.   _____

4. Our teacher _____ to swim.   _____

C   All the words in the box below begin with the letter **E.** Underline the second letter in each word. Then write the words in alphabetical order.

eraser   enormous   edge   easy   evening   escape   eggs   eyes

A   Use Reading Textbook B to answer these questions.

1. You want to find the first page in the Reading Textbook that tells about the topic **biceps.** On what page does that topic begin? _____

2. Write the first word on that page. _____

3. What is the last page on which the topic **biceps** appears? _____

4. Write the last word on that page. _____

5. You want to find the first page in the textbook that tells about the topic **jungle.** On what page does that topic begin? _____

6. Write the first word on that page. _____

7. What is the last page on which the topic **jungle** appears? _____

8. Write the last word on that page. _____

B   Write **feel** or **feels** in each sentence. Write **one** or **more than one** after each sentence.

1. She _____ sick.   _____

2. His forehead _____ hot.   _____

3. These slippers _____ like silk.   _____

4. We _____ angry about the test.   _____

5. This bed _____ too hard.   _____

6. They _____ shy about singing.   _____

7. My feet _____ sore.   _____

A

1. Jim ran very fast, but Linda ran even _____.

2. All of the turtles are slow, but Amy's turtle is the _____.

3. Jan said to Al, "Let's go to the store." So Jan and Al _____.

4. There was a man in the room. Then another man walked into the room.

   So now there are two _____.

5. When I put my left foot in the tub, I had one wet foot. Then I put my right

   foot in the tub. So now I have two _____.

6. The more you cut a moop's hair, the faster its hair grows. Bob kept cutting

   his moop's hair, so that moop's hair _____.

B   Use Reading Textbook B to answer these questions.

1. What part of the textbook gives an alphabetical listing of topics that

   appear in the book? _____

2. On what page does the topic **ocean** first appear in the textbook? _____

3. Write the first word on that page. _____

4. What's the last page on which the topic **ocean** appears? _____

5. Write the last word on that page. _____

C

  change   cabbage   dollar   coast   decide   dream   circus

A Write the missing part in each item.

1. Last week Ted lost a tooth. This week the same thing happened. So now

   Ted has two missing _____.

2. At first one child was in the sandbox. Then another child came into the

   sandbox. Now there are _____ in the sandbox.

3. We have had some hot days this summer, but today is the

   _____ day I can remember.

4. Jim said, "I will draw two pictures this week." And that is just what he did.

   He _____ two pictures.

5. In school, there were three turtles. Ed's turtle was four years old. Greg's

   turtle was five years old, so it was one year _____

   than Ed's turtle. Bonnie's turtle was 14 years old, so it was the

   _____ turtle in school.

6. Joe told his mom he would sweep the sidewalk. He started to sweep the

   sidewalk. When his sister asked him, "What are you doing?" Joe said, "I

   _____."

7. Henry had a loud voice. Tim spoke even _____ than

   Henry. Ernie spoke the _____ of all.

B

thought   ruler   tenth   rich   taste   rough   return

A

middle   island   machine   insist   mummy   money   idea

1. _____

2. _____

3. _____

4. _____

5. _____

6. _____

7. _____

A

flower   juggle   football   fence   fifty   join

1. _____

2. _____

3. _____

4. _____

5. _____

6. _____

A Draw a line from each expression to what it means.

1. She slept like a log last night. •

2. She was really hard-nosed. •

3. Well, I'll be a monkey's uncle. •

4. She talked until she was blue • in the face.

• She was tough.

• She talked a lot.

• She slept very soundly.

• The person was really surprised.

B

thirsty	notice	twice	terrible	neither	traffic	toast

1. _____

2. _____

3. _____

4. _____

5. _____

6. _____

7. _____

1. **clothing**

    A. _____

    B. _____

    C. _____

2. **tools**

    A. _____

    B. _____

    C. _____

3. **vehicles**

    A. _____

    B. _____

    C. _____

B Draw a line from each expression to what it means.

1. He was always walking on thin ice. •   • He was tough.

2. It was raining cats and dogs. •   • He was really surprised.

3. He was really hard-nosed. •   • He slept very soundly.

4. He could have been knocked •   • He does best when he faces
   over by a feather.   serious problems.

5. He slept like a log. •   • He was always doing
                                               dangerous things.

6. He always does best when •   • It was raining very hard.
   his back is against the wall.

A

| ruler | airplane | done | knives | thumb |
| dinner | ceiling | report | honest | weather |

1. _____   6. _____

2. _____   7. _____

3. _____   8. _____

4. _____   9. _____

5. _____   10. _____

B

1. fruits

    _____   _____

    _____   _____

2. vegetables

    _____   _____

    _____   _____

3. animals

    _____   _____

    _____   _____

A

| shadow | lemon | giant | visit | destroy |
| great | younger | bread | space | globe |

B

THINGS I DID

_____ day   _____ day   _____ day

1. _____

    A. _____

    B. _____

    C. _____

    D. _____

2. _____

    A. _____

    B. _____

    C. _____

    D. _____

3. _____

    A. _____

    B. _____

    C. _____

    D. _____

A

<u>face</u>	<u>fasten</u>

<u>favorite</u>	<u>field</u>

<u>figure</u>	<u>first</u>

<u>five</u>	<u>float</u>

<u>foam</u>	<u>freeze</u>

<u>friend</u>	<u>frost</u>

1. frond _____

2. fever _____

3. famous _____

4. flea _____

5. factory _____

6. finally _____

7. forest _____

8. faint _____

9. frisky _____

10. finish _____

A

label	lawyer
lazy	lifeboat
lightning	living
loaf	maggot
magic	matter
mean	meter

1. metal _____

2. list _____

3. ledge _____

4. machine _____

5. lady _____

6. manage _____

TEST 13

Test Score [   ]

A Write the name of the part of the book you would use for each item. The answer to each item is **glossary, index,** or **table of contents.**

1. You want to find out the page number for the first selection on lesson 71.

_____

2. You want to find out what the word **image** means.

_____

3. You want to find out how many selections are presented in lesson 104.

_____

B Use your dictionary to find the correct meaning of the underlined word in each sentence. Circle the correct meaning.

1. His story about what happened was <u>sincere</u>.

   • not true   • honest   • funny

2. She <u>ignited</u> the pile of tree branches.

   • collected   • cut up   • set fire to

C For each word, underline the prefix. Circle the root. Make a line over the suffix.

1. remarkable   2. dishonestly

D

• **Her cheeks were apples.**

1. What two things are the same. _____

2. How are they the same? _____

E

1. The first speech was <u>brief</u>. The second speech was not very long either.

2. Gina's dress had <u>vivid colors</u>, but her mother's was not very colorful.

3. The new <u>regulation</u> did not fit in with the other rules.

Draw a line from each word in the first column to the word that means the same thing.

1. brief •   • bright

2. vivid •   • rule

3. regulation •   • short

DID	The trail bike crash into the tree. Fred
	fell off the bike. The big noise scared
WH	the bull. Rita saw that Fred was in
WH RO	trouble. The horse galloped toward Fred
	and the horse reached him just before the
	bull did.

Check 1: Did you write sentences that give a clear picture of what must have happened in the middle picture? (WH)

Check 2: Are all your sentences written correctly? (CP, DID, RO)

Passage Editing Exercise

	The painter carried his ladder over to
RO	*the tree and he leaned the ladder against*
WH	*the tree. Mike picked some apples.*
DID	*He toss the apples to the painter. The*
CP	*painter put the apples on the ground Anita*
	unfolded the blanket. She took the food
	and drinks from the picnic basket and set
	them on the blanket.

Check 1: Did you write sentences that give a clear picture of what must have happened in the middle picture? (WH)

Check 2: Are all your sentences written correctly? (CP, DID, RO)

	The back wheel of Alicia's bike was badly
	bent. Alicia took her bike to a bike repair
RO	*shop and the repair person looked at the*
Q	*bent wheel on her bike. "He said I can fix*
	that bike in five minutes." He put the bike
WH	*on the counter. Alicia sat on a bench. She*
	read a book and drank a soda while she
DID	*waited. The bike repair person work on the*
	bike for hours. He was not able to figure
	out how to fix the wheel.

Check 1: Did you give a clear picture of what happened in the first picture? (WH)

Check 2: Did you correctly punctuate the sentence that tells what somebody said? (Q)

Check 3: Did you give a clear picture of what must have happened in the middle picture? (WH)

Check 4: Are all your sentences written correctly? (CP, RO, DID)

Passage Editing Exercise

COM	Roger was looking for monkeys in the jungle. He caught a mother monkey. After he brought the monkey to his campsite he locked it in a cage. He put the key to the cage on a table. He walked over to his cot and sat down. He said, "I finally caught that monkey. I'll take her back to the zoo." A baby monkey sat on a branch and watched what was happening.
	Roger took off his boots and laid down on the on the cot in his tent. The baby monkey climbed down the tree when Roger went to sleep. The baby monkey walked quietly to the table as Roger slept. The baby monkey took the key and opened the lock on the cage. The mother monkey walked out of the cage door after the baby monkey unlocked the cage. The monkeys grabbed some bananas from the table and climbed back up in the tree. Roger continued to sleep as the happy monkeys ate the bananas.
W–1	

Check 1: Does your first paragraph give a clear picture of what happened before the first picture and in the first picture? (WH)

Check 2: Does your second paragraph give a clear picture of what happened in the middle picture and the last picture? (WH, P)

Check 3: Did you write at least two sentences that begin with a part that tells when? (W, COM)

	The sheriff and his deputy were near the
	edge of an old wooden bridge that went
	across a stream. The sheriff was pointing
	across the stream. The deputy was
	standing behind the sheriff. The sheriff
DID	*start to walk across the bridge. As the*
	sheriff walked across the bridge, the
	deputy said, "That bridge doesn't seem
Q	*safe. After the sheriff had taken a couple*
	of steps, the bridge broke. The sheriff
	tumbled into the water. As the sheriff
COM	*climbed out of the water the deputy*
	laughed and held out his hand to help the
	sheriff.

Check 1: Do your sentences about picture 1 tell where the sheriff and his deputy were and what they were doing? (WH)

Check 2: Do your sentences for the other pictures tell what somebody or something did? (WH, DID)

Check 3: Do you have at least one sentence that begins with a part that tells when ? (W, COM)

Passage Editing Exercise **153**

RO	Sandra decided to take her dog ice skating at the pond and she rode her
	horse to the pond. Her dog followed the
	horse. When they got to the pond, Sandra
DID	climb off her horse and tied the reins to
	a nearby tree. She took off her coat and
WH	boots. Then she put four little skates on
	her dog. She picked up her dog and carried
	it through the snow to the ice.

Check 1: Did you give a clear picture of what happened in the first picture? (WH)

Check 2: Did you give a clear picture of what must have happened in the middle picture? (WH)

Check 3: Are all your sentences written correctly? (CP, DID, RO)

	Dave was working at an auto repair
CP	*shop he was changing a wheel. He told the*
	woman he was working with, "After work, I
P	*am going to the beach and cool off." When*
	Dave finished work, he rode to the beach on
	his bike. His dog ran next to the bike. When
	he got to the beach, Dave changed into his
	swimsuit. He put his uniform and shoes
	next to his bike. He took the leash off his
	dog and ran through the sand into the
DID	*water. His dog follow him. They went*
	swimming. As Dave and his dog ran through
	the water, Dave said, "I love to go
Q	*swimming on a hot day.*

Check 1: Does your first paragraph give a clear picture of what happened in the first picture? (WH)

Check 2: Does your second paragraph give a clear picture of what happened in the middle picture and the last picture? (WH, P)

Check 3: Are all your sentences written correctly? (CP, RO, DID, Q)

DID	The elephant trainer drive the truck to
WH	the side of the road. The elephants
	walked out of the truck. The elephant
	trainer led the elephants across the road.
	John took the spare tire out of the car
RO	trunk and the elephants stood behind the
WH	car. John took the flat tire off the car
	and put it on the ground. He got ready to
	put the spare tire on the back wheel.

Check 1: Did you write sentences that give a clear picture of what must have happened in the middle picture? (WH)

Check 2: Are all your sentences written correctly? (CP, DID, RO)

	Ron's boat sank near a desert island.
	Ron picked up his toolbox from the boat
CP	and stepped into the water He said,
Q	"I'll need these tools". He walked through
	the water to the beach. He opened up the
WH	toolbox and took out an ax. He used the
	tree trunks to spell the word help on the
	beach. He also used the tree trunks and
RO	some leaves to build a shelter and he sat
	and waited for help.

Check 1: Did you give a clear picture of what happened in the first picture? (WH)

Check 2: Did you correctly punctuate the sentence that tells what somebody said? (Q)

Check 3: Did you give a clear picture of what must have happened in the middle picture? (WH)

Check 4: Are all your sentences written correctly? (CP, RO, DID)

	Mrs. Hart was walking down a hill with
CP	her dog her dog was walking behind her.
	Suddenly, Mrs. Hart tripped over a rock.
DID	Her dog stopped and watch her. Mrs.
	Hart rolled down the hill towards a cliff.
	When her dog saw that Mrs. Hart was in
COM	trouble the dog started to run after her.
	Mrs. Hart rolled to the edge of the cliff.
	Just before she rolled over the edge of the
	cliff, her dog grabbed Mrs. Hart's coat and
	held onto her.

Check 1: Does your first paragraph give a clear picture of what happened before the first picture and in the first picture? (WH)

Check 2: Does your second paragraph give a clear picture of what happened in the missing picture and the last picture? (WH, P)

Check 3: Did you write at least two sentences that begin with a part that tells when? (W, COM)

	Tony and Rita were driving down the road
	in their truck when they came to a
	tunnel. The truck was too tall to get
RO	through the tunnel and Tony and Rita got
DID	out of the truck. Tony look at the tunnel.
	He said, "How can we get through this
	tunnel?" Rita bent down next to the front tire.
	As Rita looked at the front tire, she
	got an idea. She told Tony that if they let
	some air out of the tires, the truck could
	be low enough to make it through the
	tunnel. They let air out of all the tires.
CP	Then, they drove slowly through the tunnel
	the top of the truck was just low enough
WH	to get through the tunnel.

Check 1: Does your first paragraph give a clear picture of what happened before the first picture and in the first picture? (WH)

Check 2: Does your second paragraph give a clear picture of what happened in the middle picture and the last picture? (WH, P)

Check 3: Are all your sentences written correctly? (CP, RO, DID, Q)

Passage Editing Exercise   **159**

	Mr. Wingate swung the net at the
RO	butterfly and the net missed the
WH	butterfly. The mother bear growled. Mr.
	Wingate heard the growl. He ran away as
CP	fast as he could he ran towards a big tree.
	The mother bear ran after Mr. Wingate. He
DID	climb up the tree.

Check 1: Did you write sentences that give a clear picture of what must have happened in the middle picture? (WH)

Check 2: Are all your sentences written correctly? (CP, DID, RO)

	Henry and Carlos decided to go fishing
	on Saturday. Their alarm clock rang at
CP	6 in the morning the boys sat up. Carlos
	reached to turn off the alarm clock. After
	a couple of minutes, the boys got out of
WH	bed. They put the boat on the trailer and
	drove to the lake. When they arrived at the
	lake, they took the boat off the trailer and
	carried it into the water. Both boys put on
	their life jackets and got ready to go
	fishing. Carlos carried the oars into the
DID	boat and climb onto the front seat. Henry
	sat in the back seat with the fishing pole.

Check 1: Did you give a clear picture of what happened in the first picture? (WH)

Check 2: Did you give a clear picture of what must have happened in the middle picture? (WH)

Check 3: Are all your sentences written correctly? (CP, DID, RO)

	Sam and Ann were on the bank of a wide
	river. Ann was picking up rocks. Sam was
CP	watching her. Ann threw one of the rocks
	it almost went to the other side of the
WH	river. Sam picked up a rock and threw it as
	hard as he could. The rock did not go as
	far as the rock that Ann threw. Ann just
	smiled. When Sam saw that his rock did
COM	not go very far Sam said, "My arm is sore."
	Ann threw another rock. This rock went
	even further than the first rock she threw.

Check 1: Do your sentences about picture 1 tell where Sam and Ann were and what they were doing? (WH)

Check 2: Do your sentences for the other pictures tell what Sam did and what Ann did? (WH, DID)

Check 3: Do you have at least two sentences for each picture? (WH)

RO	The mother fish grabbed the fishing line in her mouth. The mother fish got angry
	and she swam away from the boat as fast
	as she could swim. Jim felt a tug on the
	fishing line. He held on to the fishing pole.
WH DID	Rhonda dropped the net and grab the oars.

Check 1: Did you write sentences that give a clear picture of what must have happened in the middle picture? (WH)

Check 2: Are all your sentences written correctly? (CP, DID, RO)

	Fred and the monkey were inside the monkey's cage. Fred was sitting on a tree
WH	stump. Fred yawned and said, "I think I'll take a nap." As Fred yawned, the monkey started to climb down the rope. In a few
CP	moments, Fred fell asleep when the monkey saw that Fred was asleep, it pushed the cage door open and walked out of the cage.
COM	When Fred woke up he looked around and said, "Where is that monkey?" The monkey sat on top of the cage and smiled.

Check 1: Do your sentences about picture 1 tell where Fred and the monkey were and what they were doing? (WH)

Check 2: Do your sentences for the other pictures tell what somebody or something did? (WH, DID)

Check 3: Do you have at least one sentence that begins with a part that tells when? (W, COM)

	The sheriff took a shower at the end
RO	of a hard day of work and a deputy came
	in to the shower room. The deputy said,
Q	"We have an emergency call. The sheriff
	got ready as fast as he could. He hurried
WH	out of the shower and grabbed a towel. He
	picked up the emergency tool kit and ran
	outside in his bare feet. He ran towards
	the police car. His deputy put a leash on
	the dog. He also grabbed the sheriff's
	shoes and socks. The deputy and the dog
DID	run after the sheriff.

Check 1: Did you give a clear picture of what happened in the first picture? (WH)

Check 2: Did you correctly punctuate the sentence that tells what somebody said? (Q)

Check 3: Did you give a clear picture of what must have happened in the middle picture? (WH)

Check 4: Are all your sentences written correctly? (CP, RO, DID)

	Henry and Carlos decided to go fishing. They set their alarm clock before they went to sleep. The boys got up when the alarm clock went off. Carlos turned off the alarm clock.
	Henry and Carlos got out of bed and got dressed. They walked outside to their truck. They put the boat on the trailer. They drove the truck to the lake. When
COM	they arrived at the lake they took the boat off the trailer and put it in the water. Both boys put on their life jackets. Carlos carried the oars into the boat and climbed onto the front seat. Henry sat in the back seat with the fishing pole. Carlos rowed to the middle of the lake. He said, "We're going to be lucky today. I bet we catch ten fish."
W–1	

Check 1: Does your first paragraph give a clear picture of what happened in the first picture? (WH)

Check 2: Does your second paragraph give a clear picture of what happened in the middle picture and the last picture? (WH, P)

Check 3: Did you write at least two sentences that begin with a part that tells when? (W, COM)

	Roger took off his boots and went to
WH	sleep on a cot inside the tent. The baby
	monkey took the key from the table and
DID	walked over to the cage. It open the lock
	with the key. The mother monkey pushed
	the cage door open and walked out of the
	cage. The two monkeys walked to the
WH	table. The monkeys climbed up the tree
CP	to a branch that was over the tent Roger
	slept the whole time.

Check 1: Did you write sentences that give a clear picture of what must have happened in the middle picture? (WH)

Check 2: Are all your sentences written correctly? (CP, DID, RO)

	When the bridge broke, Tom fell into the
	stream. He stood up in the water. He said,
Q	*"That water is cold." I am freezing." He*
CP	*climbed out of the stream he carried*
	several logs to a campfire pit and built a
	fire. He took off his wet clothes and boots.
WH	*He took a blanket from his tent and put it*
DID	*over him. He walk over to the fire to get*
	warm.

Check 1: Did you give a clear picture of what happened in the first picture? (WH)

Check 2: Did you correctly punctuate the sentence that tells what somebody said? (Q)

Check 3: Did you give a clear picture of what must have happened in the middle picture? (WH)

Check 4: Are all your sentences written correctly? (CP, RO, DID)

RO	Carla rode her bike over to the tree and she got off her bike. She leaned the bike
WH	against the tree. The monkey climbed up the tree and walked out onto a branch near the kite. The monkey shook the branches
DID	near the kite. The kite came loose. It float into the air. Carla decided to give a treat
CP	to the monkey she took out some bananas that were in the basket of her bike.

Check 1: Did you write sentences that give a clear picture of what must have happened in the middle picture? (WH)

Check 2: Are all your sentences written correctly? (CP, DID, RO)

CP	Jerry's friends had a big lunch at Jerry's house They left at 1 o'clock. The kitchen
	was a mess. Jerry's mom opened the
	kitchen door and said, "Please clean the
Q	kitchen while I go shopping. She went to
	the grocery store. Jerry worked hard while
RO	she was gone and he carried the dirty
	dishes from the table to the sink. He
WH	cleaned the table. He mopped the floor. He
	took out the garbage. He finished cleaning
	at 4 o'clock.

Check 1: Did you give a clear picture of what happened in the first picture? (WH)

Check 2: Did you correctly punctuate the sentence that tells what somebody said? (Q)

Check 3: Did you give a clear picture of what must have happened in the middle picture? (WH)

Check 4: Are all your sentences written correctly? (CP, RO, DID)

RO	Alex ran onto the thin ice and the ice
WH	broke. He could not climb out of the water.
	Sally skated over to the barricade. She
	took the long board from the barricade.
CP	She put the board on the ice she held one
	end of the board. She slid the other end
DID	to the hole in the ice. Alex climb onto the
	board.

Check 1: Did you write sentences that give a clear picture of what must have happened in the middle picture? (WH)

Check 2: Are all your sentences written correctly? (CP, DID, RO)

Passage Editing Exercise

RO Q DID	Jill had almost finished painting the porch rail and her mother came to the door. She said, "get ready for your piano lesson." Jill finish painting the rail and cleaned up her mess. She put the paint brushes in the paint cleaner. She put the lid on the paint. She also folded the rags. She took off her work boots and went
WH	inside. She sat on the piano bench with her mother.

Check 1: Did you give a clear picture of what happened in the first picture? (WH)

Check 2: Did you correctly punctuate the sentence that tells what somebody said? (Q)

Check 3: Did you give a clear picture of what must have happened in the middle picture? (WH)

Check 4: Are all your sentences written correctly? (CP, RO, DID)

	The rock hit the hornet's nest.
WH	*Hundreds of hornets came out of the*
RO	*nest and the angry hornets flew toward*
CPWH	*James. The hornets almost caught him*

Check 1: Did you write sentences that give a clear picture of what must have happened in the middle picture? (WH)

Check 2: Are all your sentences written correctly? (CP, DID, RO)

Passage Editing Exercise

	Ted was repairing a fence when he heard a car making funny noises. Mrs. Smith stood next to the car. Smoke was coming
Q	from the engine. Mrs. Smith said "Can you help me? I'm having trouble with my car."
CP	Ted tried to help he lifted up the hood. He made the engine stop smoking but could
WH	not get the car to start. Mrs. Smith steered the car as Ted pulled the car with his tractor.

Check 1: Did you give a clear picture of what happened in the first picture? (WH)

Check 2: Did you correctly punctuate the sentence that tells what somebody said? (Q)

Check 3: Did you give a clear picture of what must have happened in the middle picture? (WH)

Check 4: Are all your sentences written correctly? (CP, RO, DID)

	Tracy and Maria rode their snowmobile
	near a frozen lake. Nobody lived near this
RO	lake and the snowmobile hit a large rock
	that was covered with snow. The
	snowmobile was damaged and couldn't run.
	Maria said, "We'll freeze unless we get
P	out of the cold." The girls decided to build
	an igloo. They took the tool kit from the
WH	snowmobile. They stacked up the blocks of
	ice to make an igloo. When they were
	finished, it was snowing. As Tracy started
Q	to crawl inside the igloo, Maria said, "we'll
	be a lot warmer when we get inside."

Check 1: Does your first paragraph give a clear picture of what happened before the first picture and in the first picture? (WH)

Check 2: Does your second paragraph give a clear picture of what happened in the middle picture and the last picture? (WH, P)

Check 3: Are all your sentences written correctly? (CP, RO, DID, Q)

	Jerry and his friends were in the
	kitchen. They were eating a big lunch. They
	finished lunch at 1 o'clock. The kitchen
	was a mess. As Jerry's friends were
COM	leaving Jerry's mom opened the kitchen
	door. She said, "Please clean the kitchen
P	while I go shopping." Jerry worked hard
	while his mom went shopping for groceries.
	He carried the dirty dishes from the table
DID	to the sink. He cleaned the table. He wash
	all the dishes and put them away. He
	mopped the floor. He took out the garbage.
	He finished cleaning at 4 o'clock. His mom
	walked into the room just as he finished
	cleaning. Jerry said, "Everything is cleaned
	up. What's for dinner?"
W-1	

Additional Practice
Test 1

A   Put in the capitals and periods.

a girl threw a ball to her brother she threw the ball too hard it rolled into the street the boy started to run into the street a truck moved toward the boy a woman saw the truck she grabbed the boy the truck ran over the ball the woman told the boy to be more careful

B   Fix up the passage so that each sentence begins with a capital and ends with a period.

a man took a big egg out of a nest. The man brought the egg to his house he thought that the egg might be worth a lot of money. The doorbell rang the man walked to the door. He opened the door a big bird flew into the room. It picked up the egg the man fainted. The big bird flew away with the egg

C Fix up each sentence so that it tells what the persons did.

1. They were wearing helmets.

2. She was throwing the ball.

3. They were cleaning the room.

4. The boys were sitting on the floor.

5. He was wearing a new shirt.

6. The clown was rubbing his nose.

sat	threw	rubbed	wore	cleaned

D Fix up each sentence so that it tells what the person or thing did.

1. The boy was chasing a dog.

2. The girl was washing the car.

3. He was writing a letter.

4. She was eating apples.

5. The airplane was taking off.

took	chased	wrote	ate	washed

E Fill in the blank next to each sentence with *he, she, it* or *they*.

1. The man and the woman ate lunch.
2. Latrell and Kedrick walked on the sand.
3. The truck had a flat tire.
4. The apples cost 84 cents.
5. The woman wore a red shirt.
6. The old book was worth a lot of money.
7. Alberto and his dog went jogging.
8. The old man wore a long blue coat.

1. _____ ate lunch.
2. _____ walked on the sand.
3. _____ had a flat tire.
4. _____ cost 84 cents.
5. _____ wore a red shirt.
6. _____ was worth a lot of money.
7. _____ went jogging.
8. _____ wore a long blue coat.

F Fill in the blank next to each sentence with *he, she, it* or *they*.

1. A cat and a dog made a mess.
2. The girls went to school.
3. My mother was very pretty.
4. Rodney and his brother were not home.
5. Four ducks swam on the lake.
6. The tables were old.
7. My brother came home late.
8. That car was bright red.

1. _____ made a mess.
2. _____ went to school.
3. _____ was very pretty.
4. _____ were not home.
5. _____ swam on the lake.
6. _____ were old.
7. _____ came home late.
8. _____ was bright red.

Circle the subject of each sentence. Underline the predicate.

1. Five cats were on the roof.

2. They read two funny books.

3. A red bird landed on a roof.

4. A dog and a cat played in their yard.

5. It stopped.

Circle the subject of each sentence. Underline the predicate.

1. Sara and Harry painted the kitchen blue.

2. Sara had a paintbrush.

3. Harry used a roller.

4. They stopped to eat lunch.

5. She laughed.

6. The windows were blue.

Test 2

A Read the paragraph. Fix up any run-ons.

Nancy Wilson and Jane Robinson lived in a big city and they wanted to visit a friend who lived on a farm. The girls worked every day after school to earn money for the trip and Nancy helped Mr. Jackson fix his car. Jane helped Mr. Baker paint his apartment and then Nancy and Jane soon had enough money for the trip.

B   Read the paragraph. Fix up any run-ons.

Yuri and Bill found a little bird that had fallen out of its nest and then they took the little bird home with them. Mr. Robinson gave them a book about birds and the book told how to take care of the bird. Yuri fed the bird while Bill made a bed for it and then the bird got better. Yuri and Bill took it back to its nest.

C   Write the verb for each sentence.

1. She stopped the car.   _____

2. A young man was walking on the path.   _____

3. That truck had a flat tire.   _____

4. Linda and Sandy were eating apples.   _____

5. Everybody clapped.   _____

6. He sat near the door.   _____

D   Write the verb for each sentence.

1. She painted her room.   _____

2. They were sitting on the floor.   _____

3. His shirt was not dirty.   _____

4. He was helping his mother.   _____

5. A cow and a horse ate the grass.   _____

6. That nice woman helped us.   _____

     Additional Practice   **181**

E   Rewrite each item with an apostrophe **s.**

1. The car belonged to **my uncle.** The car had a flat tire.

   _____ had a flat tire.

2. The cat belonged to **her friend.** The cat was sleeping.

   _____ was sleeping.

3. The hat belonged to **Jill.** The hat was on the table.

   _____ was on the table.

4. The toy belonged to **the baby.** The toy was broken.

   _____ was broken.

F   Rewrite each item with an apostrophe **s.**

1. The book belonged to **Jean.** The book had two hundred pages.

   _____ had two hundred pages.

2. The glasses belonged to **my sister.** The glasses were dirty.

   _____ were dirty.

3. The shirt belonged to **the teacher.** The shirt had red and white stripes.

   _____ had red and white stripes.

4. The leg belonged to **Ray.** The leg was broken.

   _____ was broken.

G   Fill in the blanks with the correct words.

Three women worked on a house.

_____ wore work clothes.

_____ cut a board.

_____ used a saw.

_____ carried three pieces

of wood. _____ carried the

boards on her shoulder. _____ hammered nails into the wood.

H   Fill in the blanks with the correct words.

_____ and

_____ were working.

_____ were doing yard

work. _____ sawed a

branch from a tree. _____

wore a hat and work clothes.

_____ held the branch with

one hand. _____ dug a hole

in the dirt.

     Additional Practice

Test 3

A The number after each sentence tells how many mistakes. Fix up the mistakes.

1. the boys goed to Bills house. (3)

2. Alice fell asleep she was very tired. (2)

3. that boys shirt has six red buttons and four yellow buttons (3)

4. My best friends are jerry gomez and alex jordan. (4)

5. Melissa and richard put their dog on richards bed. (3)

6. We looked outside and The rain had just stopped. (2)

B

1. My dads cat had four kittens (2)

2. She teached robert and jerry how to ride a bike. (3)

3. she washed the windows of her dads car (3)

4. We seen mrs. jordan in the store she waved to us. (5)

and

_____ and

_____ were swimming.

_____ wore a bathing cap.

_____ also wore a watch.

_____ sat near the water.

_____ wore sunglasses.

_____ stood next to the

blanket. _____ wore shorts.

_____ read a book.

_____ and _____ picked apples from

a tree. _____ wore a hat. _____ had a

beard. _____ stood on a box. _____ held a

bucket. _____ and _____ sat on a blanket.

_____ read a book. _____ wore a shirt with the

number 9 on the back. _____ drew a picture.

Additional Practice **185**

E   Circle the subject in each sentence.
Write **P** in front of each sentence that has a pronoun for a subject.

_____ 1. The tree was beautiful.

_____ 2. He ate pizza for dinner.

_____ 3. Those dogs chased our cat.

_____ 4. Tina read a book.

_____ 5. It fell off the table.

_____ 6. They bought new shirts.

_____ 7. My sister painted the room.

_____ 8. Robert finished his homework.

F   Circle the subject in each sentence.
Write **P** in front of each sentence that has a pronoun for a subject.

_____ 1. Linda's shirt was dirty.

_____ 2. They painted the door.

_____ 3. He is ten years old.

_____ 4. A new girl walked into our class.

_____ 5. It had big tires.

_____ 6. A boy and his friend went to the store.

_____ 7. My little brother is seven years old.

_____ 8. She walked to school.

G Put in an apostrophe if the underlined object belongs to someone.

1. six <u>chairs</u>

2. my fathers <u>chairs</u>

3. my fathers <u>chair</u>

4. some <u>apples</u>

5. that trees <u>leaves</u>

6. a cars <u>headlights</u>

7. a boys <u>kites</u>

8. two big <u>oranges</u>

9. those red <u>cars</u>

10. that boys <u>books</u>

11. the teachers <u>pencil</u>

12. the tallest <u>girls</u>

H Put in an apostrophe if the underlined object belongs to someone.

1. a girls <u>hairbrush</u>

2. that cats <u>tail</u>

3. the birds in the <u>tree</u>

4. the bugs on the <u>table</u>

5. those cats near <u>John</u>

6. an old mans <u>face</u>

7. the womans <u>umbrella</u>

8. many <u>cups</u>

9. a girls <u>suitcase</u>

Test 4

A   Write **N** above each noun.
Write **P** above each pronoun.
Write **V** above each verb.

1. They talked to her.

2. A little cat sat next to him.

3. The rain made them sad.

4. He saw it.

B   Write **N** above each noun.
Write **P** above each pronoun.
Write **V** above each verb.

1. Linda helped him.

2. They were next to her.

3. My teacher saw it.

4. That new book helped them.

The number after each item tells how many mistakes are in the item. Fix up the mistakes.

1. James said, Today is my birthday. We are having a party. (2)

2. Bill met Alice in the park. She said you look good. (4)

3. Anns dad is very tall he plays basketball. (3)

4. The doctor said you have a bad cold. Don't go outside. (4)

5. I seen ann and jane at Mr. jordans house. (5)

D The number after each item tells how many mistakes are in the item. Fix up the mistakes.

1. Mr. roberts said "That is his bike. (3)

2. the boys went to Bills house. (2)

3. that boys shirt has six red buttons and four yellow buttons (3)

4. My best friends are jerry gomez and alex jordan. (4)

5. Melissa and richard put their dog on richards bed. (3)

6. He said I am hungry. I want an apple (4)

Test 5

A Write **N** above each underlined noun.
Write **P** above each underlined pronoun.
Write **V** above each underlined verb.

1. He bought a new shirt at the store.

2. Yesterday morning, we saw her.

3. My school had a big playground.

4. A girl painted her room.

B Write **N** above each underlined noun.
Write **P** above each underlined pronoun.
Write **V** above each underlined verb.

1. She stood in front of the table.

2. In the morning, she ate an apple.

3. The water dripped on it.

4. After the party, she walked to her house.

C For each sentence, circle the subject and underline the whole predicate.

1. Before the sun went down, the birds began to sing.

2. Jason and Robert fell asleep after a few minutes.

3. After school, we walked home.

4. Last night, everybody went to sleep early.

5. We had eggs for breakfast.

D For each sentence, circle the subject and underline the whole predicate.

1. When the light turned green, she put her foot on the gas pedal.

2. After dinner, my dad took a nap.

3. He felt very tired when he got home.

4. Before school, we played on the bars.

5. My brother and my sister were at school.

E For each sentence, fill in the blank with the word **asked** or the word **said.** Then make the correct ending mark.

1. Her friend _____, "That was a good meal   "

2. Jane _____, "Did it rain   "

3. He _____, "Are you hungry   "

4. Jason _____, "Nobody is home   "

F For each sentence, fill in the blank with the word **asked** or the word **said.** Then make the correct ending mark.

1. He _____, "Is lunch ready   "

2. They _____, "Did you see her   "

3. Alice _____, "Where is Adams Avenue   "

4. He _____, "It's time to eat   "

G Put a comma in each sentence that begins with the part that tells when.

1. The boys went home after school.

2. During the rainstorm our dog hid under the bed.

3. After we fixed the car we made dinner.

4. In the morning Jane walked to school.

5. That girl was happy when she got her report card.

6. He fell asleep while he read a book.

7. After James sat down the music started.

H Put a comma in each sentence that begins with the part that tells when.

1. A cat jumped up when the alarm clock rang.

2. When we got home the dog started barking.

3. In the morning we ate breakfast.

4. While the baby slept we talked quietly.

5. Her brother was happy when he got the letter.

6. They finished the job just before midnight.

7. Before they made lunch the cooks washed their hands.

Test 7

A Write **V** above each verb.
Write **N** above each noun.
Write **A** above each adjective.

1. Four cats slept on the big pillow.

2. An old man drove a new car.

3. That smart girl knew every answer.

B Write **V** above each verb.
Write **N** above each noun.
Write **A** above each adjective.

1. A young boy jumped into the deep water.

2. Her uncle had a friendly dog.

3. Tom helped his little sister.

C Fix up each sentence so it is punctuated correctly.

1. The flag was red white and blue. (1)

2. My brother my mother and my sister had colds. (1)

3. James opened the door put on his coat and walked down the stairs. (1)

D Fix up each sentence so it is punctuated correctly.

1. We found two bottles three cans and six coins. (1)

2. Raymond his sister and Carmen went skating. (1)

3. Jean turned off the radio closed the window and turned on the heater. (1)

E Capitalize all parts of any item that names one person or one place.

1. a big city

2. burnside avenue

3. bumpo car company

4. that lake

5. mississippi river

6. dr. Mitchell

7. an old house

8. los angeles

F Capitalize all parts of any item that names one person or one place.

1. my sister

2. oak street

3. new york

4. united states

5. this country

6. his street

7. dr. evans

8. delto stove company

G Fill in each blank with the verb **was** or **were.**

1. Sandy and her mother _____ on the bus.

2. She _____ on the bus.

3. The girl's arm _____ sore.

4. You _____ wise to buy that book.

5. Three men _____ in the boat.

Fill in each blank with the verb **was** or **were.**

1. Ellen's son _____ sick.

2. You _____ wrong.

3. They _____ at school.

4. James and I _____ in the house.

5. The boy's teacher _____ happy.

6. You _____ first in line.

Test 8

A Write **V** above each verb. Write **N** above each noun. Write **P** above each pronoun. Write **A** above each adjective.

1. When the bell rang, we went to our classroom.

2. Linda stood in front of a large desk.

3. That tiny black fly flew into my cup.

4. During the night, a strong wind blew.

B

1. During the big storm, we went inside an old house.

2. He saw many black ants on the kitchen table.

3. Two old men helped her.

4. His truck moved slowly up a steep hill.

5. After the meeting, she went to the store.

Additional Practice

The number after each sentence tells how many mistakes. Fix up the mistakes.

1. The mississippi river is the longest river in the united states. (4)

2. Texas alaska and california are the biggest states. (3)

3. Is los angeles bigger than san francisco? (4)

4. We lived on baldwin street until last september. (3)

5. After she brushed her teeth. She went to bed. (2)

6. My favorite cities are new york dallas and miami. (5)

7. Ann asked mr. james Where can i buy that book (7)

D

1. The empire state building is in new york. (5)

2. Robert fed the dog washed the dishes and cleaned his room before lunch. (1)

3. Is mexico larger than canada (3)

4. Jill asked, "Where is Dr. Lees office? (2)

5. I bought apples oranges and pears at the store. (1)

6. December january and february are the coldest months of the year. (3)

7. Yokos sister lives on washington street. (3)

8. Tom and his sister was in the park. (1)

Test 9

1. Write the date for the fifth day of August in the year 1968.

_____

2. Write the date for the third day of June in the year 2001.

_____

3. Write the date for the eleventh day of March in the year 1792.

_____

4. Write the date for the eighth day of July in the year 1812.

_____

5. Write the date for the nineteenth day of November in the year 1947.

_____

B

1. Write the date for the 21st day of May in the year 1886.

_____

2. Write the date for the seventeenth day of September in the year 2010.

_____

3. Write the date for the tenth day of January in the year 1935.

_____

4. Write the date for the 23rd day of March in the year 1722.

_____

Additional Practice

1. Greenville Iowa _____

2. Street number: 45
   Street name: Vine Street
   City name: Greenville
   State name: Iowa

Write the address with commas.

_____

3. Street number: 7
   Street name: Old Goat Road
   City name: Chico
   State name: California

Write the address with commas.

_____

Test 11

A Write **sing** or **sings** in each blank. Write **one** or **more than one** after each sentence.

1. His dad _____ well.   _____

2. His dad and mom _____ well.   _____

3. Those ten kids _____ well.   _____

4. Her older brothers _____ well.   _____

B Write **like** or **likes** in each blank. Write **one** or **more than one** after each sentence.

1. My friend's dad _____ spinach.   _____

2. The women _____ to fish.   _____

3. They _____ our cat.   _____

4. She _____ to run.   _____